DATA PREPROCESSING
WITH **PYTHON** FOR
ABSOLUTE BEGINNERS

Step-by-Step Guide
with Hands-on Projects
and Exercises

AI PUBLISHING

How to contact us

If you have any feedback, please let us know by sending an email to contact@aipublishing.io.

Your feedback is immensely valued, and we look forward to hearing from you. It will be beneficial for us to improve the quality of our books.

To get the Python codes and materials used in this book, please click the link below:

www.aipublishing.io/book-preprocessing-python

The order number is required.

About the Publisher

At AI Publishing Company, we have established an international learning platform specifically for young students, beginners, small enterprises, startups, and managers who are new to data sciences and artificial intelligence.

Through our interactive, coherent, and practical books and courses, we help beginners learn skills that are crucial to developing AI and data science projects.

Our courses and books range from basic introduction courses to language programming and data sciences to advanced courses for machine learning, deep learning, computer vision, big data, and much more, using programming languages like Python, R, and some data science and AI software.

AI Publishing's core focus is to enable our learners to create and try proactive solutions for digital problems by leveraging the power of AI and data sciences to the maximum extent.

Moreover, we offer specialized assistance in the form of our free online content and eBooks, providing up-to-date and useful insight into AI practices and data science subjects, along with eliminating the doubts and misconceptions about AI and programming.

Our experts have cautiously developed our online courses and kept them concise, short, and comprehensive so that you can understand everything clearly and effectively and start practicing the applications right away.

We also offer consultancy and corporate training in AI and data sciences for enterprises so that their staff can navigate through the workflow efficiently.

With AI Publishing, you can always stay closer to the innovative world of AI and data sciences.

If you are eager to learn the A to Z of AI and data sciences but have no clue where to start, AI Publishing is the finest place to go.

Please contact us by email at: contact@aipublishing.io.

AI Publishing Is Searching for Authors Like You

Interested in becoming an author for AI Publishing? Please contact us at author@aipublishing.io.

We are working with developers and AI tech professionals just like you, to help them share their insights with the global AI and Data Science lovers. You can share all your knowledge about hot topics in AI and Data Science.

An Important Note to Our Valued Readers:

Download the Color Images

Our print edition books are available only in black & white at present. However, the digital edition of our books is available in color PDF.

We request you to download the PDF file containing the color images of the screenshots/diagrams used in this book here:

www.aipublishing.io/book-preprocessing-python

The typesetting and publishing costs for a color edition are prohibitive. These costs would push the final price of each book to $50, which would make the book less accessible for most beginners.

We are a small company, and we are negotiating with major publishers for a reduction in the publishing price. We are hopeful of a positive outcome sometime soon. In the meantime, we request you to help us with your wholehearted support, feedback, and review.

For the present, we have decided to print all of our books in black & white and provide access to the color version in PDF. This is a decision that would benefit the majority of our readers, as most of them are students. This would also allow beginners to afford our books.

Get in Touch with Us

Feedback from our readers is always welcome.

For general feedback, please send us an email
at contact@aipublishing.io and
mention the book title in the subject of your message.

Although we have taken every care to ensure the accuracy
of our content, mistakes do happen. If you have found
a mistake in this book, we would be grateful if you could
report this to us as soon as you can.

If you are interested in becoming an AI Publishing author
and if there is a topic that you have expertise in
and you are interested in either writing or contributing
to a book, please send us an email
at author@aipublishing.io.

Table of Contents

Preface

§ Book Approach

The book follows a very simple approach. It is divided into nine chapters. Chapter 1 introduces the basic concept of data preprocessing, along with the installation steps for the software that we will need to perform data preprocessing in this book. Chapter 1 also contains a crash course on Python. A brief overview of different data types is given in Chapter 2. Chapter 3 explains how to handle missing values in the data, while the categorical encoding of numeric data is explained in Chapter 4. Data discretization is presented in Chapter 5. Chapter 6 explains the process of handling outliers, while Chapter 7 explains how to scale features in the dataset. Handling of mixed and datetime data type is explained in Chapter 8, while data balancing and resampling has been explained in Chapter 9. A full data preprocessing final project is also available at the end of the book.

In each chapter, different types of data preprocessing techniques have been explained theoretically, followed by practical examples. Each chapter also contains an exercise that students can use to evaluate their understanding of the concepts explained in the chapter. The Python notebook for each chapter is provided in the resources. It is advised that instead of copying the code, you write the code yourself, and in case of an error, you match your code with the corresponding Python notebook, find and then correct the error. The datasets used in this book are either downloaded at runtime or are available in the *Resources/Datasets* folder.

§ Data Science and Data preprocessing

Data science and data preprocessing are two different but interrelated concepts. Data science refers to the science of extracting and exploring data in order to find patterns that can be used for decision making at different levels. Data preprocessing is the process of preprocessing data in a way that can convey useful information that can be used as input to various data science processes such as data visualization, machine learning, deep learning, etc.

This book is dedicated to data preprocessing and explains how to perform different data preprocessing techniques on a variety of datasets using various data preprocessing libraries written in the Python programming language. It is suggested that you use this book for data preprocessing purposes only and not for data science or machine learning. For the application of data preprocessing in data science and machine learning, read this book in conjunction with dedicated books on machine learning and data science.

§ Who Is This Book For?

This book explains the process of data preprocessing using various libraries from scratch. Hence, the book is aimed ideally at absolute beginners to data preprocessing. Though a background in the Python programming language and feature engineering can help speed up learning, the book contains a crash course on Python programming language in the first chapter. Therefore, the only prerequisite to efficiently using this book is access to a computer with internet. All the codes and datasets have been provided. However, to download data preprocessing libraries, you will need internet.

In addition to beginners to data preprocessing with Python, this book can also be used as a reference manual by intermediate and experienced programmers as it contains data preprocessing code samples using multiple data visualization libraries.

§ How to Use This Book?

As I said earlier, the data preprocessing techniques and concepts taught in this book have been divided into multiple chapters. To get the best out of this book, I would suggest that you first get your feet wet with the Python programming language, especially the object-oriented programming concepts. To do so, you can take a crash course on Python in chapter 1 of this book. Also, try to read the chapters of this book in order since concepts taught in subsequent chapters are based on previous chapters. In each chapter, try to first understand the theoretical concepts behind different types of data preprocessing techniques and then try to execute the example code. I would again stress that rather than copy and pasting code, try to write the code yourself, and in case of any error, you can match your code with the source code provided in the book as well as in the Python notebooks in the resources. Finally, try to answer the questions in the exercises at the end of each chapter. The solutions to the exercises have been given at the end of the book.

To facilitate the reading process, occasionally, the book presents three types of box-tags in different colors: Requirements, Further Readings, and **Hands-on Time**. Examples of these boxes are shown below.

> **Requirements**
>
> This box lists all requirements needed to be done before proceeding to the next topic. Generally, it works as a checklist to see if everything is ready before a tutorial.

> **Further Readings**
>
> Here, you will be pointed to some external reference or source that will serve as additional content about the specific **Topic** being studied. In general, it consists of packages, documentations, and cheat sheets.

> **Hands-on Time**
>
> Here, you will be pointed to an external file to train and test all the knowledge acquired about a **Tool** that has been studied. Generally, these files are Jupyter notebooks (.ipynb), Python (.py) files, or documents (.pdf).

The box-tag Requirements lists the steps required by the reader after reading one or more topics. **Further Readings** provides relevant references for specific topics to get to know the additional content of the topics. **Hands-on Time** points to practical tools to start working on the specified topics. Follow the instructions given in the box-tags to get a better understanding of the topics presented in this book.

About the Author

M. Usman Malik has a Ph.D. in Computer Science from Normandy University, France, with Artificial Intelligence and Machine Learning being the main areas of research. Usman Malik has over five years of industry experience in Data Science and has worked with both private and public sector organizations. In his free time, he likes to listen to music and play snooker.

Warning

In Python, indentation is very important. Python indentation is a way of telling a Python interpreter that the group of statements belongs to a particular code block. After each loop or if-condition, be sure to pay close attention to the intent.

Example

```python
# Python program showing
# indentation

site = 'aisciences'

if site == 'aisciences':
    print('Logging to www.aisciences.io...')
else:
    print('retype the URL.')
print('All set !')
```

To avoid problems during execution, we advise you to download the codes available on Github by requesting access from the link below. Please have your order number ready for access:

www.aipublishing.io/book-preprocessing-python

1

Introduction

1.1. What is Data Preprocessing?

With the huge amount of data at disposal, more and more researchers and industry professionals are finding ways to use this data for research and commercial benefits. However, most of the data available by default is too raw. It is important to preprocess data before it can be used to identify important patterns or can be used to train statistical models that can be used to make predictions.

Data Preprocessing is the process of cleaning and engineering data in a way that it can be used as input to several important data science tasks such as data visualization, machine learning, deep learning, and data analytics.

Some of the most common data Preprocessing tasks include feature engineering, feature scaling, outlier detection, handling missing values, categorical variable encoding, data discretization, etc. You will see all of these concepts in detail in this chapter, with the help of various examples implemented in the Python programming language.

In this chapter, you will see how to set up the Python environment needed to run various data visualization libraries.

The chapter also contains a crash Python course for absolute beginners in Python. Finally, the different data Preprocessing libraries that we are going to study in this book have been discussed. The chapter ends with a simple exercise.

1.2. Environment Setup

1.2.1. Windows Setup

The time has come to install Python on Windows using an IDE. In fact, we will use Anaconda throughout this book right from installing Python to writing multithreaded codes in the coming lectures. Now, let us get going with the installation.

This section explains how you can download and install Anaconda on Windows.

To download and install Anaconda, follow these steps.

1. Open the following URL in your browser.

    https://www.anaconda.com/distribution/

2. The browser will take you to the following webpage. Select the latest version of Python (3.8 at the time of writing this book). Now, click the *Download* button to download the executable file. Depending upon the speed of your internet, the file will download within 2-3 minutes.

Anaconda 2019.07 for Windows Installer

Python 3.7 version

Download

64-Bit Graphical Installer (486 MB)
32-Bit Graphical Installer (418 MB)

Python 2.7 version

Download

64-Bit Graphical Installer (427 MB)
32-Bit Graphical Installer (361 MB)

3. Run the executable file after the download is complete. You will most likely find the downloaded file in your download folder. The name of the file should be similar to "Anaconda3-5.1.0-Windows-x86_64." The installation wizard will open when you run the file, as shown in the following figure. Click the *Next* button.

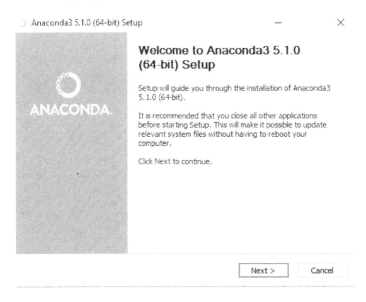

4. Now click *I Agree* on the *License Agreement* dialog, as shown in the following screenshot.

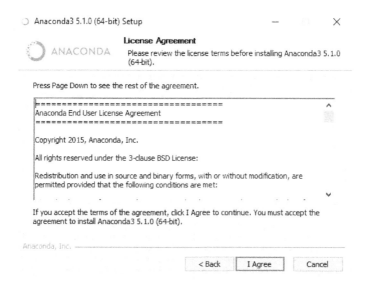

5. Check the *Just Me* radio button from the *Select Installation Type* dialogue box. Click the *Next* button to continue.

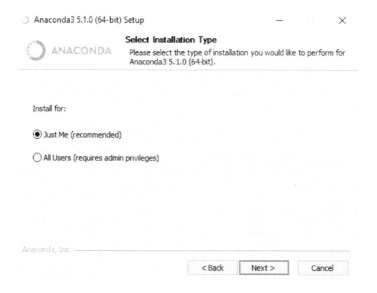

6. Now, the *Choose Install Location* dialog will be displayed. Change the directory if you want, but the default is preferred. The installation folder should at least have 3

GB of free space for Anaconda. Click the *Next* button.

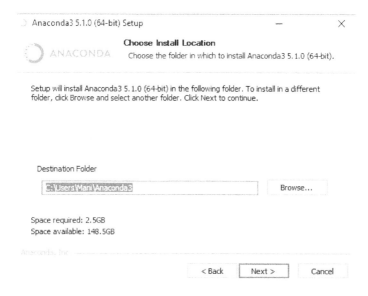

7. Go for the second option, *Register Anaconda as my default Python 3.8* in the *Advanced Installation Options* dialogue box. Click the *Install* button to start the installation, which can take some time to complete.

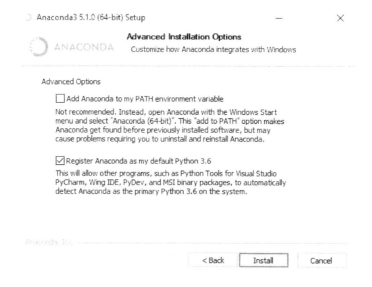

8. Click *Next* once the installation is complete.

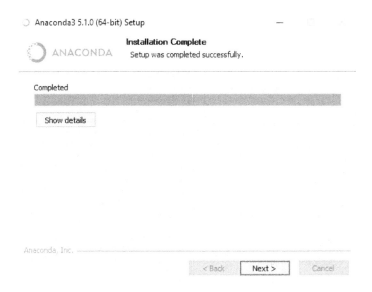

9. Click *Skip* on the *Microsoft Visual Studio Code Installation* dialog box.

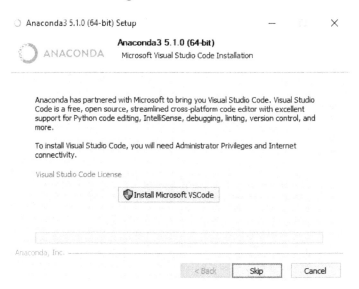

10. You have successfully installed Anaconda on your Windows. Excellent job. The next step is to uncheck both checkboxes on the dialog box. Now, click on the *Finish* button.

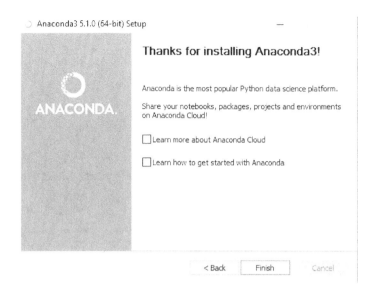

1.2.2. Mac Setup

Anaconda's installation process is almost the same for Mac. It may differ graphically, but you will follow the same steps you followed for Windows. The only difference is that you have to download the executable file, which is compatible with the Mac operating system.

This section explains how you can download and install Anaconda on Mac.

To download and install Anaconda, follow these steps.

1. Open the following URL in your browser.

    https://www.anaconda.com/distribution/

2. The browser will take you to the following webpage. Select the latest version of Python for Mac (3.8 at the time of writing this book). Now, click the *Download* button to download the executable file. Depending

upon the speed of your internet, the file will download within 2–3 minutes.

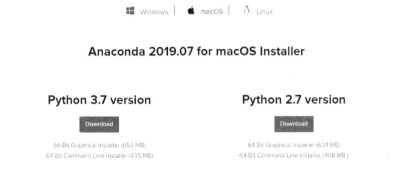

3. Run the executable file after the download is complete. You will most likely find the downloaded file in your download folder. The name of the file should be similar to "Anaconda3-5.1.0-Windows-x86_64." The installation wizard will open when you run the file, as shown in the following figure. Click the *Continue* button.

4. Now click *Continue* on the *Welcome to Anaconda 3 Installer* window, as shown in the following screenshot.

5. The *Important Information* dialog will pop up. Simply click *Continue* to go with the default version that is Anaconda 3.

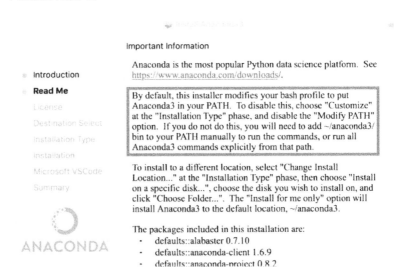

6. Click *Continue* on the *Software License Agreement* Dialog.

7. It is mandatory to read the license agreement and click the *Agree* button before you can click the *Continue* button again.

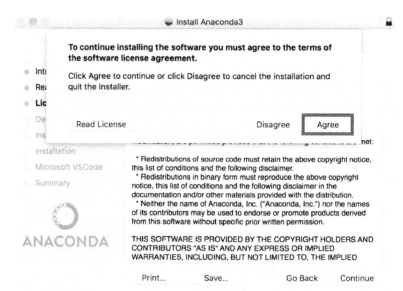

8. Simply click *Install* on the next window that appears.

The system will prompt you to give your password. Use the same password you use to login to your Mac computer. Now, click on *Install Software*.

9. Click *Continue* on the next window. You also have the option to install Microsoft VSCode at this point.

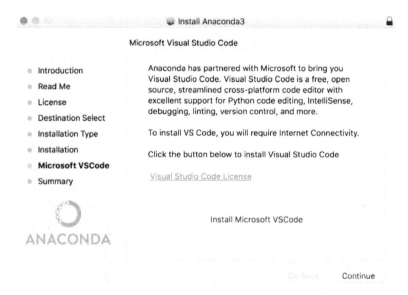

The next screen will display the message that the installation has completed successfully. Click on the *Close* button to close the installer.

There you have it. You have successfully installed Anaconda on your Mac computer. Now, you can write Python code in Jupyter and Spyder the same way you wrote it in Windows.

1.2.3. Linux Setup

We have used Python's graphical installers for installation on Windows and Mac. However, we will use the command line to install Python on Ubuntu or Linux. Linux is also more resource-friendly, and the installation of this software is particularly easy as well.

Follow these steps to install Anaconda on Linux (Ubuntu distribution).

1. Go to the following link to copy the installer bash script from the latest available version.

    https://www.anaconda.com/distribution/

Anaconda 2019.07 for Linux Installer

Python 3.7 version   **Python 2.7 version**

Download   Download

64-Bit (x86) Installer (617 MB)   64-Bit (x86) Installer (476 MB)
64-Bit (Power8 and Power9 Installer (326 MB)   64-Bit (Power8 and Power9 Installer (208 MB)

2. The second step is to download the installer bash script. Log into your Linux computer and open your terminal. Now, go to /temp directory and download the bash you downloaded from Anaconda's home page using curl.

```
$ cd / tmp

$ curl -o https://repo.anaconda.com.archive/
Anaconda3-5.2.0-Linux-x86_64.sh
```

3. You should also use the cryptographic hash verification through SHA-256 checksum to verify the integrity of the installer.

```
$ sha256sum Anaconda3-5.2.0-Linux-x86_64.sh
```

You will get the following output.

```
09f53738b0cd3bb96f5b1bac488e5528df9906be2480fe61df40e0e0d19e3d48
Anaconda3-5.2.0-Linux-x86_64.sh
```

4. The fourth step is to run the Anaconda Script, as shown in the following figure.

```
$ bash Anaconda3-5.2.0-Linux-x86_64.sh
```

The command line will produce the following output. You will be asked to review the license agreement. Keep on pressing **Enter** until you reach the end.

```
Output

Welcome to Anaconda3 5.2.0

To continue the installation process, kindly review the
license agreement.
Please press Enter to continue
>>>
...
Do you approve the license terms? [yes|No]
```

Type *Yes* when you get to the bottom of the License Agreement.

5. The installer will ask you to choose the installation location after you agree to the license agreement.

Simply press **Enter** to choose the default location. You can also specify a different location if you want.

```
Output

Anaconda3 will now be installed on this location:
/home/tola/anaconda3

- Press ENTER to confirm the location
- Press CTRL-C to abort the installation
- Or specify a different location below

[/home/tola/anaconda3] >>>
```

The installation will proceed once you press **Enter.** Once again, you have to be patient as the installation process takes some time to complete.

6. You will receive the following result when the installation is complete. If you wish to use conda command, type *Yes.*

```
Output
...
Installation finished.
Do you wish the installer to prepend Anaconda3 install
location to path in your /home/tola/.bashrc? [yes|no]
[no]>>>
```

At this point, you will also have the option to download the Visual Studio Code. Type *yes* or *no* to install or decline, respectively.

7. Use the following command to activate your brand new installation of Anaconda3.

```
$ source `/.bashrc
```

8. You can also test the installation using the conda command.

```
$ conda list
```

Congratulations! You have successfully installed Anaconda on your Linux system.

1.3. Python Crash Course

If you are familiar with the elementary concepts of the Python programming language, you can skip this section. For those who are absolute beginners to Python, this section provides a brief overview of some of the most basic concepts of Python. Python is a vast programming language, and this section is by no means a substitute for a complete Python book. However, if you want to see how various operations and commands are executed in Python, you are welcome to follow along the rest of this section.

1.3.1. Writing Your First Program

You have already installed Python on your computer and established a unique environment in the form of Anaconda. Now, it is time to write your first program, that is the Hello World!

In order to write a program in Anaconda, you have to launch the Anaconda Navigator. Search *Anaconda Navigator* in your Windows Search Box. Now, click on the Anaconda Navigator application icon, as shown in the following figure.

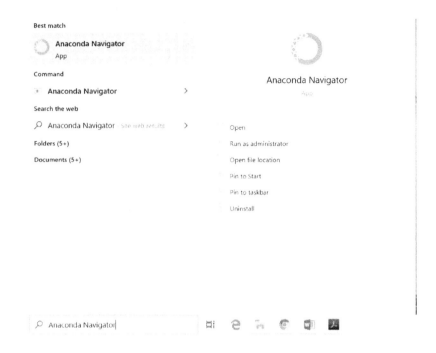

Once you click on the application, the Anaconda's dashboard will open. The dashboard offers you a myriad of tools to write your code. We will use the *Jupyter Notebook*, the most popular of these tools, to write and explain the code throughout this book.

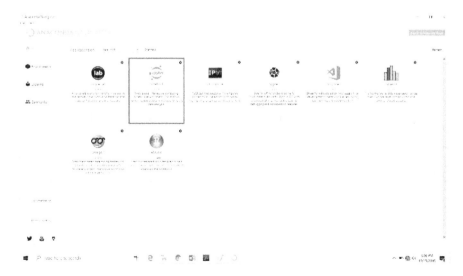

The Jupyter Notebook is available at second from the top of the dashboard. You can use Jupyter Notebook even if you don't have access to the internet as it runs right in your default browser. Another method to open Jupyter Notebook is to type *Jupyter Notebook* in the Window's search bar. Subsequently, click on the Jupyter Notebook application. The application will open in a new tab on your browser.

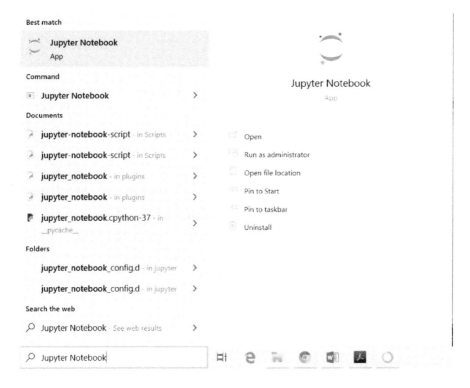

The top right corner of Jupyter Notebook's own dashboard houses a *New* button, which you have to click to open a new document. A dropdown containing several options will appear. Click on *Python 3*.

A new Python notebook will appear for you to write your programs. It looks as follows.

Jupyter Notebook consists of cells, as evident from the above image, making its layout simple and straightforward. You will write your code inside these cells. Let us write our first ever Python program in Jupyter Notebook.

1.3.1. Writing Your First Program

```
print("Welcome to Data Preprocessing with Python")
Welcome to Data Preprocessing with Python
```

The above script basically prints a string value in the output using the print() method. The print() method is used to print on the console any string passed to it. If you see the following output, you have successfully run your first Python program.

Output:

```
Welcome to Data Visualization with Python
```

Let's now explore some of the other important Python concepts starting with Variables and Data Types.

Requirements – Anaconda, Jupyter, and Matplotlib

- All the scripts in this book have been executed via the Jupyter notebook. Therefore, you should have the Jupyter notebook installed.
- The Numpy and Pandas, and Matplotlib libraries should also be installed before this chapter.

Hands-on Time – Source Codes

All IPython notebook for the source code of all the scripts in this chapter can be found in Codes/Chapter 1.ipynb file from the book resources I would suggest that you write all the code in this chapter yourself and see if you can get the same output as mentioned in this chapter.

1.3.2. Python Variables and Data Types

Data types in a programming language refers to the type of data that the language is capable of processing. The following are the major data types supported by Python.

a. Strings
b. Integers
c. Floating Point Numbers
d. Booleans
e. Lists

f. Tuples

g. Dictionaries

A variable is an alias for the memory address where actual data is stored. The data or the values stored at a memory address can be accessed and updated via the variable name. Unlike other programming languages like C++, Java, and C#, Python is loosely typed, which means that you don't have to state the data type while creating a variable. Rather, the type of data is evaluated at runtime.

The following example demonstrates how to create different data types and how to store them in their corresponding variables. The script also prints the type of the variables via the **type()** function.

Script 1:

```
# A string Variable
first_name = "Joseph"
print(type(first_name))

# An Integer Variable
age = 20
print(type(age))

# A floating point variable
weight = 70.35
print(type(weight))

# A boolean variable
married = False
print(type(married))

#List
cars = ["Honda", "Toyota", "Suzuki"]
print(type(cars))
```

```
#Tuples
days = ("Sunday", "Monday", "Tuesday", "Wednesday",
"Thursday", "Friday", "Saturday")
print(type(days))

#Dictionaries
days2 = {1:"Sunday", 2:"Monday", 3:"Tuesday", 4:"Wednesday",
5:"Thursday", 6:"Friday", 7:"Saturday"}
print(type(days2))
```

Output:

```
<class 'str'>
<class 'int'>
<class 'float'>
<class 'bool'>
<class 'list'>
<class 'tuple'>
<class 'dict'>
```

1.3.3. Python Operators

Python programming language contains the following types of operators:

a. Arithmetic Operators

b. Logical Operators

c. Comparison Operators

d. Assignment Operators

e. Membership Operators

Let's briefly review each of these types of operators.

Arithmetic Operators

Arithmetic operators are used to perform arithmetic operations in Python. The following table sums up the arithmetic operators supported by Python. Suppose X = 20 and Y = 10.

Operator Name	Symbol	Functionality	Example
Addition	+	Adds the operands on either side	X + Y= 30
Subtraction	−	Subtracts the operands on either side	X − Y = 10
Multiplication	*	Multiplies the operands on either side	X * Y= 200
Division	/	Divides the operand on the left by the one on right	X / Y= 2.0
Modulus	%	Divides the operand on the left by the one on right and returns remainder	X % Y= 0
Exponent	**	Takes exponent of the operand on the left to the power of right	X ** Y = $1024 \times e^{10}$

Here is an example of arithmetic operators with output:

Script 2:

```
X = 20
Y = 10
print(X + Y)
print(X - Y)
print(X * Y)
print(X / Y)
print(X ** Y)
```

Output:

```
30
10
200
2.0
10240000000000
```

Logical Operators

Logical operators are used to perform logical AND, OR, and NOT operations in Python. The following table summarizes the logical operators. Here, X is True, and Y is False.

Operator	Symbol	Functionality	Example
Logical AND	and	The condition becomes true if both the operands are true.	(X and Y) = False
Logical OR	or	The condition becomes true if any of the two operands are true.	(X or Y) = True
Logical NOT	not	Used to reverse the logical state of its operand.	not(X and Y) =True

Here is an example that explains the usage of the Python logical operators.

Script 3:

```
X = True
Y = False
print(X and Y)
print(X or Y)
print(not(X and Y))
```

Output:

```
False
True
True
```

Comparison Operators

Comparison operators, as the name suggests, are used to compare two or more than two operands. Depending upon the relation between the operands, comparison operators return Boolean values. The following table summarizes comparison operators in Python. Here, X is 20, and Y is 35.

Operator	Symbol	Description	Example
Equality	==	If the values of both the operands are equal, then the condition returns true.	(X == Y) = false
Inequality	!=	If the values of both the operands are not equal, then the condition returns true.	(X = Y) = true
Greater than	>	If the value of the left operand is greater than the right one, then the condition returns true.	(X> Y) = False
Smaller than	<	Returns true if value of the left operand is smaller than the right one.	(X< Y) = True
Greater than or equal to	>=	If the value of the left operand is greater than or equal to the right one, then the condition returns true.	(X > =Y) = False
Smaller than or equal to	<=	Returns true if value of the left operand is smaller than or equal to the right one	(X<= Y) = True

The comparison operators have been demonstrated in action in the following example:

Script 4:

```
X = 20
Y = 35

print(X == Y)
print(X != Y)
print(X > Y)
print(X < Y)
print(X >= Y)
print(X <= Y)
```

Output:

```
False
True
False
True
False
True
```

Assignment Operators

Assignment operators are used to assign values to variables. The following table summarizes the assignment operators. Here, X is 20, and Y is equal to 10.

Operator	Symbol	Description	Example
Assignment	=	Used to assign value of the right operand to the right.	R = X+ Y assigns 30 to R
Add and assign	+=	Adds the operands on either side and assigns the result to the left operand	X += Y assigns 30 to X
Subtract and assign	-=	Subtracts the operands on either side and assigns the result to the left operand	X -= Y assigns 10 to X

Multiply and Assign	*=	Multiplies the operands on either side and assigns the result to the left operand	X *= Y assigns 200 to X
Divide and Assign	/=	Divides the operands on the left by the right and assigns the result to the left operand	X/= Y assigns 2 to X
Take modulus and assign	%=	Divides the operands on the left by the right and assigns the remainder to the left operand	X %= Y assigns 0 to X
Take exponent and assign	**=	Takes exponent of the operand on the left to the power of right and assign the remainder to the left operand	X **= Y assigns $1024 \times e^{10}$ to X

Take a look at script 6 to see Python assignment operators in action.

Script 5:

```
X = 20; Y = 10
R = X + Y
print(R)

X = 20;
Y = 10
X += Y
print(X)

X = 20;
Y = 10
X -= Y
print(X)
```

```
X = 20;
Y = 10
X *= Y
print(X)

X = 20;
Y = 10
X /= Y
print(X)

X = 20;
Y = 10
X %= Y
print(X)

X = 20;
Y = 10
X **= Y
print(X)
```

Output:

```
30
30
10
200
2.0
0
10240000000000
```

Membership Operators

Membership operators are used to find if an item is a member of a collection of items or not. There are two types of membership operators. They are the in operator and the not in operator. The following script shows the in operator in action.

Script 6:

```
days = ("Sunday", "Monday", "Tuesday", "Wednesday",
"Thursday", "Friday", "Saturday")
print('Sunday' in days)
```

Output:

```
True
```

And here is an example of the not in operator.

Script 7:

```
days = ("Sunday", "Monday", "Tuesday", "Wednesday",
"Thursday", "Friday", "Saturday")
print('Xunday' not in days)
```

Output:

```
True
```

1.3.4. Conditional Statements

Conditional statements are used to implement conditional logic in Python. Conditional statements help you decide whether to execute a certain code block or not. There are three chief types of conditional statements in Python:

    a. If statement

    b. If-else statement

    c. If-elif statement

IF Statement

If you have to check for a single condition and you do not concern about the alternate condition, you can use the if statement. For instance, if you want to check if 10 is greater than 5, and based on that you want to print a statement, you can use the if statement. The condition evaluated by the if statement returns a Boolean value. If the condition evaluated by the if statement is true, the code block that follows the if statement executes. It is important to mention that in Python, a new code block starts at a new line with the on tab indented from the left when compared with the outer block.

Here, in the following example, the condition 10 > 5 is evaluated, which returns true. Hence, the code block that follows the if statement executes, and a message is printed on the console.

Script 8:

```
# The if statment

if 10 > 5:
    print("Ten is greater than 10")
```

Output:

```
Ten is greater than 10
```

IF-Else Statement

The If-else statement comes handy when you want to execute an alternate piece of code in case the condition for the if statement returns false. For instance, in the following example, the condition 5 < 10 will return false. Hence, the code block that follows the else statement will execute.

Script 9:

```
# if-else statement

if 5 > 10:
    print("5 is greater than 10")
else:
    print("10 is greater than 5")
```

Output:

```
10 is greater than 5
```

IF-Elif Statement

The `if-elif` statement comes handy when you have to evaluate multiple conditions. For instance, in the following example, we first check if 5 > 10, which evaluates to false. Next, an `elif` statement evaluates the condition 8 < 4, which also returns false. Hence, the code block that follows the last `else` statement executes.

Script 10:

```
#if-elif and else

if 5 > 10:
  print("5 is greater than 10")
elif 8 < 4:
  print("8 is smaller than 4")
else:
  print("5 is not greater than 10 and 8 is not smaller than
4")
```

Output:

```
5 is not greater than 10 and 8 is not smaller than 4
```

1.3.5. Iteration Statements

Iteration statements, also known as loops, are used to iteratively execute a certain piece of code. There are two main types of iteration statements in Python.

 a. For loop

 b. While Loop

For Loop

The for loop is used to iteratively execute a piece of code for a certain number of times. You should use for loop when you know exactly the number of iterations or repetitions for which you want to run your code. A for loop iterates over a collection of items. In the following example, we create a collection of five integers using the range() method. Next, a forloop iterates five times and prints each integer in the collection.

Script 11:

```
items = range(5)
for item in items:
print(item)
```

Output:

```
0
1
2
3
4
```

While Loop

The while loop keeps executing a certain piece of code unless the evaluation condition becomes false. For instance, the while loop in the following script keeps executing unless variable c becomes greater than 10.

Script 12:

```
c = 0
while c < 10:
    print(c)
c = c +1
```

Output:

```
0
1
2
3
4
5
6
7
8
9
```

1.3.6. Functions

Functions, in any programming language, are used to implement that piece of code that is required to be executed numerous times at different locations in the code. In such cases, instead of writing long pieces of codes again and again, you can simply define a function that contains the piece of code, and then you can call the function wherever you want in the code.

The def keyword is used to create a function in Python, followed by the name of the function and opening and closing parenthesis.

Once a function is defined, you have to call it in order to execute the code inside a function body. To call a function, you simply have to specify the name of the function, followed by opening and closing parenthesis. In the following script, we create a function named `myfunc,` which prints a simple statement on the console using the `print()` method.

Script 13:

```
def myfunc():
  print("This is a simple function")

### function call
myfunc()
```

Output:

```
This is a simple function
```

You can also pass values to a function. The values are passed inside the parenthesis of the function call. However, you must specify the parameter name in the function definition, too. In the following script, we define a function named myfuncparam(). The function accepts one parameter, i.e., num. The value passed in the parenthesis of the function call will be stored in this num variable and will be printed by the print() method inside the myfuncparam() method.

Script 14:

```
def myfuncparam(num):
  print("This is a function with parameter value: "+num)

### function call
myfuncparam("Parameter 1")
```

Output:

```
This is a function with parameter value:Parameter 1
```

Finally, a function can also return values to the function call. To do so, you simply have to use the return keyword, followed by the value that you want to return. In the following script, the myreturnfunc() function returns a string value to the calling function.

Script 15:

```
def myreturnfunc():
  return "This function returns a value"

val = myreturnfunc()
print(val)
```

Output:

```
This function returns a value
```

1.3.7. Objects and Classes

Python supports object-oriented programming (OOP). In OOP, any entity that can perform some function and have some attributes is implemented in the form of an object.

For instance, a car can be implemented as an object since a car has some attributes such as price, color, model and can perform some functions such as drive car, change gear, stop the car, etc.

Similarly, a fruit can also be implemented as an object since a fruit has a price, name, and you can eat a fruit, grow a fruit, and perform functions with a fruit.

To create an object, you first have to define a class. For instance, in the following example, a class Fruit has been defined. The class has two attributes name and price, and one method eat_fruit(). Next, we create an object f of class Fruit and then call the eat_fruit() method from the f object. We also access the name and price attributes of the f object and print them on the console.

Script 16:

```
class Fruit:

    name = "apple"
    price = 10

    def eat_fruit(self):
        print("Fruit has been eaten")


f = Fruit()
f.eat_fruit()
print(f.name)
print(f.price)
```

Output:

```
Fruit has been eaten
apple
10
```

A class in Python can have a special method called a *constructor.* The name of the constructor method in Python is __init__(). The constructor is called whenever an object of a class is created. Look at the following example to see the constructor in action.

Script 17:

```
class Fruit:

    name = "apple"
    price = 10

    def __init__(self, fruit_name, fruit_price):
        Fruit.name = fruit_name
        Fruit.price = fruit_price

    def eat_fruit(self):
        print("Fruit has been eaten")
```

```
f = Fruit("Orange", 15)
f.eat_fruit()
print(f.name)
print(f.price)
```

Output:

```
Fruit has been eaten
Orange
15
```

Further Readings – Python [1]

To study more about Python, please check Python 3 Official Documentation. Get used to searching and reading this documentation. It is a great resource of knowledge.

1.4. Different Libraries for Data Preprocessing

Owing to the growing importance of data preprocessing, several Python libraries have been developed. Some of these libraries have been briefly reviewed in this section.

1.4.1. NumPy

NumPy is one of the most commonly used libraries for numeric and scientific computing. NumPy is extremely fast and contains support for multiple mathematical domains such as linear algebra, geometry, etc. It is extremely important to learn NumPy in case you plan to make a career in data science and data preprocessing.

1.4.2. Scikit Learn

Scikit learn, also called sklearn, is an extremely useful library for machine learning in Python. Sklearn contains many built-in modules that can be used to perform data preprocessing tasks such as feature engineering, feature scaling, outlier detection, discretization, etc. You will be using Sklearn a lot in this book. Therefore, it can be a good idea to study sklearn before you start coding using this book.

1.4.3. Matplotlib

Data visualization is an important precursor to data preprocessing. Before you actually apply data preprocessing techniques on the data, you should know how the data looks like, what is the distribution of a certain variable, etc. Matplotlib is the de facto standard for static data visualization in Python.

1.4.4. Seaborn

Seaborn library is built on top of the Matplotlib library and contains all the plotting capabilities of Matplotlib. However, with Seaborn, you can plot much more pleasing and aesthetic graphs with the help of Seaborn default styles and color palettes.

1.4.5. Pandas

Pandas library, like Seaborn, is based on the Matplotlib library and offers utilities that can be used to plot different types of static plots in a single line of codes. With Pandas, you can import data in various formats such as CSV (Comma Separated View) and TSV (Tab Separated View), and can plot a variety of data visualizations via these data sources.

Further Readings – Data Preprocessing Libraries

To study more about data preprocessing libraries for Python, check these links:

Numpy [1] (https://numpy.org/)
Scikit Learn [2] (https://scikit-learn.org/stable/)
Matplotlib [3] (https://matplotlib.org/)
Seaborn [4] (https://seaborn.pydata.org/)
Pandas [5] (https://pandas.pydata.org/)

Hands-on Time – Exercise

Now, it is your turn. Follow the instruction in **the exercises below** to check your understanding of the advanced data visualization with Matplotlib. The answers to these questions are given at the end of the book.

Exercise 1.1

Question 1:

Which iteration should be used when you want to repeatedly execute a code specific number of times?

    A For Loop

    B While Loop

    C Both A and B

    D None of the above

Question 2:

What is the maximum number of values that a function can return in Python?

    A Single Value

    B Double Value

    C More than two values

    D None

Question 3:

Which of the following membership operators are supported by Python?

    A In

    B Out

    C Not In

    D Both A and C

Exercise 1.2

Print the table of integer 9 using a while loop:

§ References

1. https://numpy.org/
2. https://scikit-learn.org/
3. https://matplotlib.org/
4. https://seaborn.pydata.org/index.html
5. https://pandas.pydata.org/

2

Understanding Data Types

2.1. Introduction

A dataset can contain variables of different types depending upon the data they store. It is important to know the different types of data that a variable can store since different techniques are required to handle data of various types. In this chapter, you will see the different data types that you may come across.

2.1.1. What Is a Variable?

Before we look into a variable of different data types, let's first define what a variable is.

"A variable is an entity which stores a value that corresponds to a characteristic, quantity, or a number that can be counted or measured."

Following are some of the examples of variables:

- Name (Jon, Mike, Alen, etc.)
- Age (50, 60, 52, etc.)
- Gender (Male, Female, etc.)
- Nationality (American, British, Indian, etc.)

- Date of Birth (10-10-1990, 12-03-1983, etc.)

You can see that a variable can hold data of different types, including numeric, string, date, etc.

2.1.2. Data Types

Broadly, the data can be categorized into the following types:

1. Numerical data
2. Categorical data
3. Date and Time Variables
4. Mixed Variables

Numerical data can be further divided into two types: Discrete and Continuous data. On the other hand, the Categorical data can be divided into three main types: Nominal, Ordinal, and Date/Time data.

2.2. Numerical Data

Numerical data is a type of data that consists of numbers. Numerical data can be further divided into two types: Discrete and Continuous.

The discrete data variables are those variables that store a whole number. For instance, the number of children of a person can be 2, 3, 4, or any discrete number. You cannot say that he has 2 and a half children. Similarly, the number of cars that a person owns or the number of siblings of a person is also a discrete number. All these are discrete numerical values.

On the other hand, continuous data variables are those variables that hold continuous values, such as the amount in a person's bank account, which can be $2560.04. Similarly, the weight of a vegetable, which can be 2.5kg, or the price of a car, which can be $4057.34.

Let's now explore some examples of numerical data from the real-world dataset, i.e., Titanic Dataset.

The Titanic dataset is a famous dataset that contains information about the passengers who were on board the unfortunate *Titanic* ship that sank in 1912.

It is important to mention that before you run the script to import the Titanic dataset, or for that matter, any dataset, you need to install a few Python libraries. To do so, you have to execute the following script on your command prompt or Anaconda prompt, depending on the Python environment that you have installed on your system.

```
pip install pandas
pip install numpy
pip install matplotlib
pip install seaborn
```

Next, execute the following script to import the Titanic dataset:

Script 1:

```
import matplotlib.pyplot as plt
import seaborn as sns

plt.rcParams["figure.figsize"] = [8,6]
sns.set_style("darkgrid")

titanic_data = sns.load_dataset('titanic')

titanic_data.head()
```

The script above first imports the Matplotlib and the Seaborn libraries. It then increases the size of the default plot and then sets the grid style to dark. Finally, the above dataset uses the

load_dataset() method of the Seaborn library to import the built-in Titanic dataset. Finally, the first five rows of the Titanic dataset have been displayed. Here is the output of the script above:

	survived	pclass	sex	age	sibsp	parch	fare	embarked	class	who	adult_male	deck	embark_town	alive	alone
0	0	3	male	22.0	1	0	7.2500	S	Third	man	True	NaN	Southampton	no	False
1	1	1	female	38.0	1	0	71.2833	C	First	woman	False	C	Cherbourg	yes	False
2	1	3	female	26.0	0	0	7.9250	S	Third	woman	False	NaN	Southampton	yes	True
3	1	1	female	35.0	1	0	53.1000	S	First	woman	False	C	Southampton	yes	False
4	0	3	male	35.0	0	0	8.0500	S	Third	man	True	NaN	Southampton	no	True

You can see that the dataset contains information about the gender, age, fare, class, etc. of the passengers. Let's now identify the columns containing the discrete and continuous numerical values.

2.2.1. Discrete Data

Take a look at the *pclass* column. This column contains information about the class in which the passengers traveled. The *pclass* column can have three possible values 1, 2, and 3 corresponding to the 1st, 2nd, and 3rd class in which the passengers traveled. Since a passenger cannot travel in 1.5 class or 2.5 class, we can say that the *pclass* column contains discrete numerical values. Let's plot a bar plot that displays the count of the passengers traveling in each of the three classes:

Script 2:

```
sns.countplot(x='pclass', data=titanic_data)
```

The output shows that around 200 passengers traveled in the first class while an overwhelming majority of passengers traveled in the 3rd class of the *Titanic.*

Output:

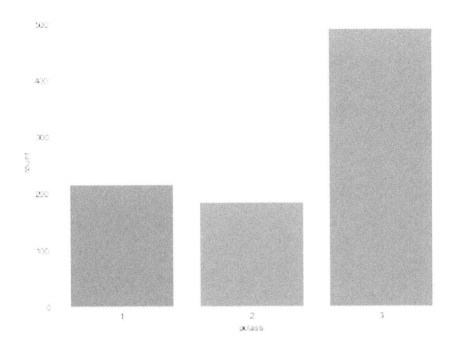

2.2.2. Continuous Data

As discussed earlier, continuous numerical data contains continuous information where data can contain fractions. In the Titanic dataset, the fare column contains continuous numerical data since fair can be in fractions. In fact, if you look at the fare paid by the customer in the first record, you can see the fare value is 7.2500, which is a continuous numerical value.

Let's plot a distributional plot for the fare column to see how the fare is distributed. Execute the following script:

Script 3:

```
sns.distplot(tips_data['fare'], kde = False)
```

Output:

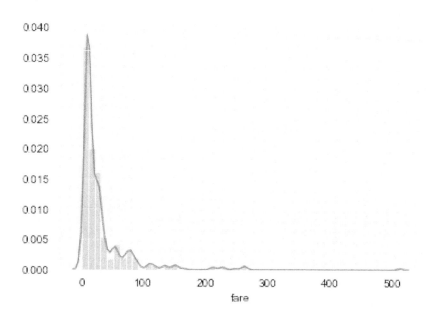

The output suggests that the majority of the passengers paid fare between 0–20 dollars.

2.2.3. Binary Data

There is one more type of numerical data called binary numerical data. Binary numerical data, as the name suggests, can only have one of the two possible values, i.e., 0 or 1. In the Titanic dataset, the survived column contains binary numerical data. The survived column shows if a passenger survived the *Titanic* crash or not. Let's plot a frequency count for the passengers who survived and for those who did not. Execute the following script:

Script 4:

```
sns.countplot(x='survived', data=titanic_data)
```

Output:

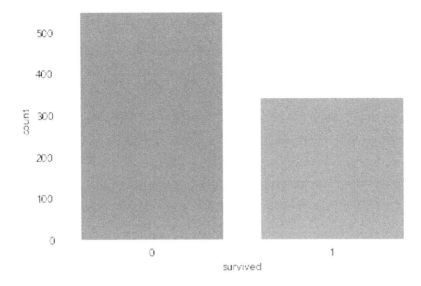

The output shows that out of around 900 passengers, around 350 survived, while around 550 couldn't survive as the bar plot for 0 shows a value of around 550.

2.3. Categorical Data

Categorical data is a type of data where values are selected from a predefined set. For instance, the gender of a person is a categorical variable since it can have only one of the two predefined values, i.e., male and female (or gender-neutral). Similarly, another example of a categorical variable is the nationality of a person, or the name of the company that makes cars, etc.

Categorical data can be further divided into two types:

1. Ordinal Data
2. Nominal Data

2.3.1. Ordinal Data

Ordinal data is a type of categorical data where values are meaningfully ordered and have some relationship between them. For instance, if the height variable can have three values, i.e., short, medium, and tall, we can say that the height variable has ordinal data since short is shorter than medium and medium is shorter than tall. In other words, the values are in a certain order. Similarly, grades of a student on a particular exam is also an ordinal variable if the grades can be A, B, C, D since grade A is better than grade B and grade B is better than grade C. There is a certain order between the values.

If you look at the Titanic dataset, you can see that the *class* column contains ordinal data. The *class* column can have three possible values, i.e., First, Second, and Third. Here there is a certain relationship between the three values. The first class is more expensive than the second class, and the second class is more expensive than the third class. We can verify this by plotting the average fare paid by the passengers in each class.

Script 5:

```
sns.barplot(x='class', y='fare', data=titanic_data)
```

Output:

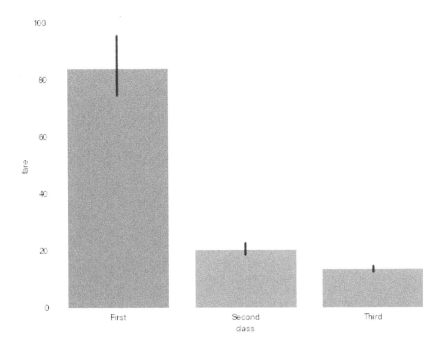

You can see that the average fare paid by the first-class passengers is around 85, while the second and third-class passengers paid average fares of 20 and 16, respectively.

2.3.2. Nominal Data

Nominal data is a type of data where values have no meaningful ordering. For instance, the nationality of a person is totally unrelated to the nationality of another person. If you look at the Titanic dataset, the embark_town column contains nominal data because the town of embarkation of different passengers does not have any relationship between them. Let's plot the average of the passengers who embarked from different towns.

Script 6:

```
sns.barplot(x='embark_town', y='age', data=titanic_data)
```

Output:

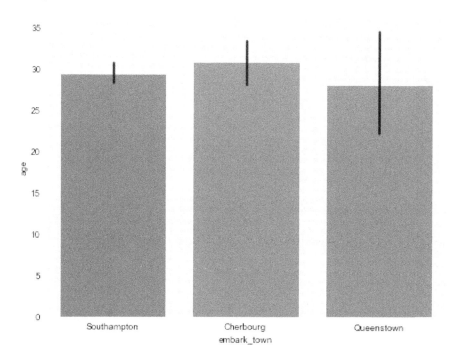

The output shows that the average ages of passengers who embarked from different towns are between 25–35.

It is important to mention that, in some cases, the categorical variables are encoded as numbers. For instance, the survived column of the Titanic dataset contains information about whether or not a passenger survived. The survived column is logically a nominal categorical variable as it can only have one of the two values. However, the values in the categorical column have been encoded as 1 and 0. Similarly, sometimes you will see that the days of the week are encoded by numbers 1 to 7.

2.4. Date and Time Data

The date and time variable can consist of date and time, date only, and time only. The following are some of the examples of the date and time variables.

1. The date of birth of a person (e.g., 10-12-1995, December 10, 1995, 10th December 1995).

2. The date and time of a football match (e.g., 11:30 am, December 10, 2021).

3. The time at which the office closes (e.g.,5:00 pm).

It is important to mention that the date and time variables can be in a variety of formats, and, therefore, a complete chapter has been dedicated to understanding date and time type data.

2.5. Mixed Data Type

Mixed data type variables are those variables that have either numerical and categorical data in different observations exclusively or contain numerical and categorical data in single observations of a data column.

For instance, if there is a column that shows the number of years a person has been married. The column can have numeric values such as 10, 12, 15, and it can also have values such as never-married, divorced, etc. So, one column here contains both numeric as well as categorical data, but a single observation here only contains either numeric or categorical data.

On the other hand, if there is a column which shows the quantity of the product bought by the customer. The column can have values such as 2 kilograms, 5 gallons, 4 dozens, etc. Here, the quantity variable has both numerical and categorical data in a single observation.

2.6. Missing Values

Missing values, as the name suggests, are those observations in the dataset that doesn't contain any value. Missing values can totally change the data patterns, and, therefore, it is extremely important to understand why missing values occur in the dataset and how to handle them. In this section, we will see the reasons behind the occurrence of missing values and their disadvantages. In the next chapter, you will see the different techniques with examples to handle missing values with the Python programming language.

2.6.1. Causes of Missing Data

There can be several reasons for missing values in the dataset. Some of them are as follows:

1. Sometimes the data is intentionally not stored by humans, which results in missing values. For instance, consider a scenario in which you are creating a dataset via a survey where users enter data. Users may or may not enter data in all the fields. In such cases, you won't get information for all the fields in the dataset.

2. Another reason behind the missing value can be the unavailability of the data in the observation being used

for feature engineering. For instance, you want to create a column that shows the area of a house. The area can be calculated by multiplying values from the length and width column. In case the length or the width for a certain observation is missing, the area column will have a null value for that particular observation.

3. Finally, calculation issues can also result in missing values. For instance, you want to insert a value in a column that results from a division of two numbers. If the denominator is zero, the result will be infinity, i.e., a missing value.

2.6.2. Disadvantages of Missing Data

There are many disadvantages of having missing data in your dataset. They are as follows:

1. Many advanced machine learning libraries, e.g., Scikit Learn doesn't work with missing values in your dataset. Therefore, missing values have to be removed from the dataset, or they have to be converted into numbers using missing data imputation techniques.

2. The problem with missing data imputation techniques is that they result in distorted data as they are not a replacement for original data.

3. Finally, distorted data may affect statistical model performances.

2.6.3. Mechanism Behind Missing Values

Earlier, we saw the general reasons behind missing values. In this section, you will study the mechanisms that are involved in generating missing values. There are three basic mechanisms:

1. Missing Data Completely at Random:

When the missing observations do not have any relation with any other column in the dataset, we can say that data has been missed randomly. For instance, in a dataset, if you cannot find the city of a person, it is missed totally randomly, and you cannot logically find the reason behind the missing value.

2. Missing Data Randomly

If the missing observations in a particular column have a relation with any other column, we can say that the data is randomly missing from these columns. For instance, females are more likely to not reveal their ages compared to males. Therefore, you are likely to find more missing values in the age column for women, compared to men, and hence, we can say that the values are randomly missing.

3. Missing Data Not Randomly

In this case, you can attribute the missing data to a logical reason. For instance, research shows that depressed patients are more likely to leave empty fields in forms compared to patients who are not depressed. Therefore, the missing data here is not randomly missed. There has been an established reason behind the missing data.

2.7. Cardinality in Categorical Data

As mentioned earlier, categorical columns contain observations where values can be any of the predefined set of labels. The cardinality of data or a data column refers to the number of unique categories or labels in the column. For instance, if you look at the *sex* column of the Titanic dataset, it can only have two possible values, i.e., male and female. Therefore, the cardinality of the sex column in the Titanic dataset will be 2. Similarly, the *class* column can have three unique values. Therefore, the cardinality of the *class* column is three.

Another extremely important consideration that you should keep in mind is that statistical algorithms work with numbers. And most of the advanced machine learning libraries, such as Scikit Learn, needs data for numbers in the output. Therefore, you will have to encode your categorical data into numbers before you can create statistical models via machine learning. The dimensionality of the dataset after encoding the categorical data depends upon the encoding scheme. We will see categorical variable encoding in detail in an upcoming chapter.

Another important point to consider when dealing with cardinality is that some labels occur more frequently than others. While training machine learning models, the train and test should have equal representation of all the labels in the output. In case a label exists only in the training set, the model will suffer overfitting during the training phase. Else, if labels don't exist in the training set and the model comes across such labels in the test set, the model will make wrong predictions since it won't be trained with the unknown labels in the training set. The same is true for rare labels.

2.8. Probability Distribution

Another extremely important concept that you should know while preparing your data is the concept of probability distribution. A probability distribution is a function that tells us the likelihood of obtaining the possible values that a variable can take. For example, the likelihood of a person having black hair is greater than blue hair. The probability distribution function is defined as:

Z= p(x)

In the above function, the probability distribution function tells us the likelihood that after the event, Z will have a specific value of X. The sum of probabilities of all the possible values of X must be equal to 1.

There are two main types of probability distribution:

1. Uniform Distribution

Uniform distribution is a type of distribution where all observations have an equal likelihood of occurrence. The plot of a uniform distribution is a straight horizontal line.

2. Normal Distribution

On the other hand, the normal distribution, which is also known as the Gaussian distribution, is a type of distribution where most of the observations occur around the center peak. And the probabilities for values further away from the peak decrease equally in both directions and have an equal likelihood of occurrence. Normal distribution usually looks like a reverse bell.

You can find the probability distribution using a histogram. Let's find the probability distribution of the tips paid by customers at a fictional restaurant. First, we will import the Tips dataset, as shown below:

Script 7:

```
tips_data = sns.load_dataset('Tips')
tips_data.head()
```

	total_bill	tip	sex	smoker	day	time	size
0	16.99	1.01	Female	No	Sun	Dinner	2
1	10.34	1.66	Male	No	Sun	Dinner	3
2	21.01	3.50	Male	No	Sun	Dinner	3
3	23.68	3.31	Male	No	Sun	Dinner	2
4	24.59	3.61	Female	No	Sun	Dinner	4

Script 8:

```
plt.title('Tip distribution')
plt.hist(tips_data[«tip»])
```

Output:

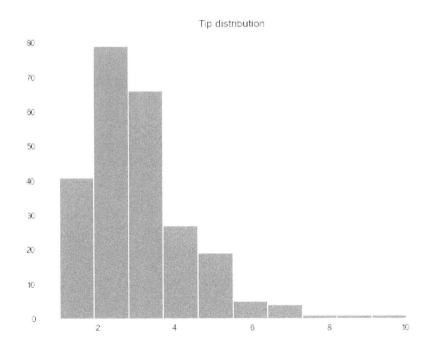

The output shows a skewed bell. This is called positively skewed distribution since the plot is stretched to the positive side of the mean.

2.9. Outliers

Outliers are the values that are too far from the rest of the observations in the columns. For instance, if the weight of most of the people in a sample varies between 50–100 kilograms, an observation of 500 kilograms will be considered as an outlier since such an observation occurs rarely.

Outliers can occur due to various reasons. For instance, if you access your online bank account from a particular city 95 percent of the time, an online check-in to your account from another city will be considered as an outlier. Such an outlier can be helpful as it can identify online frauds. However, outliers can also occur due to technical faults, human errors, machine readability, etc. In such cases, the outliers should be removed from the dataset. We will discuss outlier handling in detail in another chapter.

The best way to visualize outliers is by plotting box plots. The following script plots a box plot for the *age* column of the Titanic dataset.

Script 9:

```
sns.boxplot( y='age', data=titanic_data)
```

Output:

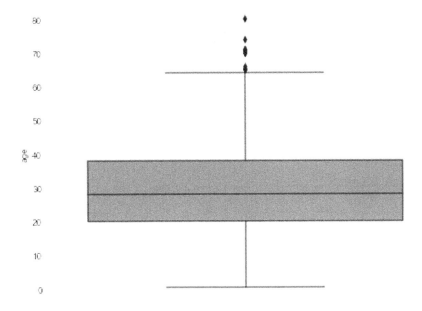

The Seaborn box plot plots the quartile information along with the outliers. Here, the above output shows that the median value of age is around 29 for all the passengers in the Titanic dataset. The 4th quartile contains values between 39 and 65 years. Beyond the age of 65, you can see outliers in the form of black dots. That means that there are few passengers beyond the age of 65.

Further Readings – More on Probability Distributions

To study more about probability distributions, take a look at this resource. (https://bit.ly/3y7QsaY)

Hands-on Time – Exercise

Now, it is your turn. Follow the instruction in **the exercises below** to check your basic understanding of data types. The answers to these questions are given at the end of the book.

Exercise 2.1

Question 1:

What is the type of *alone* column in the Titanic dataset?

A. Ordinal

B. Continuous

C. Discrete

D. Nominal

Look at the following dataset. It is called the Tips dataset. Question 2–4 are based on this Tips dataset:

	total_bill	tip	sex	smoker	day	time	size
0	16.99	1.01	Female	No	Sun	Dinner	2
1	10.34	1.66	Male	No	Sun	Dinner	3
2	21.01	3.50	Male	No	Sun	Dinner	3
3	23.68	3.31	Male	No	Sun	Dinner	2
4	24.59	3.61	Female	No	Sun	Dinner	4

Question 2:

What is the type of *day* column in the above dataset?

A. Ordinal

B. Continuous

C. Discrete

D. Nominal

Question 3:

Identify the continuous numerical columns in the Tips dataset.

Question 4:

Write the names of the discrete columns in the Tips dataset:

Question 5:

Which plot should be plotted to visualize the probability distribution in a dataset?

A. Bar Plot

B. Histogram

C. Box Plot

D. Line Plot

Question 6:

The rare label occurrence in a categorical variable can cause _____ in the training set.

A. Wrong Predictions

B. Overfitting

C. Underfitting

D. None of the above

3

Handling Missing Data

3.1. Introduction

In the previous chapters, you were introduced to many high-level concepts that we are going to study in this book. One of the concepts was missing values. You studied what missing values are, how missing values are introduced in datasets, and how they affect statistical models. In this chapter, you will see how to basically handle missing values.

3.2. Complete Case Analysis

Complete case analysis (CCA), also known as list-wise deletion, is the most basic technique for handling missing data. In CCA, you simply move all the rows or records where any column or field contains a missing value. Only those records are processed where an actual value is present for all the columns in the dataset. CCA can be applied to handle both numerical and categorical missing values.

The following table contains fictional record of patients in a hospital.

Name	Age	Gender	Blood Group
Jon	25	Male	O+
James		Male	A+
Mike	62	Male	
Nick	42	Male	B-
Harry	45	Male	AB+
Sally	26	Female	
Laura	35	Female	B+

In the table above, the age of patient James is missing, while the blood groups for patients Mike and Sally are missing. If we use the CCA approach to handle these missing values, we will simply remove the records with missing values, and we will have the following dataset:

Name	Age	Gender	Blood Group
Jon	25	Male	O+
Nick	42	Male	B-
Harry	45	Male	AB+
Laura	35	Female	B+

Advantages of CCA

The assumption behind the CCA is data is missing at random. CCA is extremely simple to apply, and no statistical technique is involved. Finally, the distribution of the variables is also preserved.

Disadvantages of CCA

The major disadvantage of CCA is that if a dataset contains a large number of missing values, a large subset of data will be removed by CCA. Also, if the values are not missing randomly, CCA can create a biased dataset. Finally, statistical models trained on a dataset on which CCA is applied are not capable of handling missing values in production.

As a rule of thumb, if you are sure that the values are missing totally at random and the percentage of records with missing values is less than 5 percent, you can use CAA to handle those missing values.

In the next sections, we will see how to handle missing numerical and categorical data.

3.3. Handling Missing Numerical Data

In the previous chapter, you studied different types of data that you are going to encounter in your data science career. One of the most commonly occurring data type is the numeric data, which consists of numbers. To handle missing numerical data, we can use statistical techniques. The use of statistical techniques or algorithms to replace missing values with statistically generated values is called imputation.

3.3.1. Mean or Median Imputation

Mean or median imputation is one of the most commonly used imputation techniques for handling missing numerical data. In mean or median imputation, missing values in a column are replaced by the mean or median of all the remaining values in that particular column.

For instance, if you have a column with the following data:

Age
15
NA
20
25
40

In the above Age column, the second value is missing. Therefore, with mean and median imputation, you can replace the second value with either the mean or median of all the other values in the column. For instance, the following column contains the mean of all the remaining values, i.e., 25 in the second row. You could also replace this value with the median if you want.

Age
15
25
20
25
40

Let's see a practical example of mean and median imputation. We will import the Titanic dataset and find the columns that contain missing values. Then, we will apply mean and median imputation to the columns containing missing values, and finally, we will see the effect of applying mean and median imputation to the missing values.

You do not need to download the Titanic dataset. If you import the Seaborn library, the Titanic data will be downloaded with it. The following script imports the Titanic dataset and displays its first five rows.

Script 1:

```
import matplotlib.pyplot as plt
import seaborn as sns

plt.rcParams["figure.figsize"] = [8,6]
sns.set_style("darkgrid")

titanic_data = sns.load_dataset('titanic')

titanic_data.head()
```

Output:

	survived	pclass	sex	age	sibsp	parch	fare	embarked	class	who	adult_male	deck	embark_town	alive	alone
0	0	3	male	22.0	1	0	7.2500	S	Third	man	True	NaN	Southampton	no	False
1	1	1	female	38.0	1	0	71.2833	C	First	woman	False	C	Cherbourg	yes	False
2	1	3	female	26.0	0	0	7.9250	S	Third	woman	False	NaN	Southampton	yes	True
3	1	1	female	35.0	1	0	53.1000	S	First	woman	False	C	Southampton	yes	False
4	0	3	male	35.0	0	0	8.0500	S	Third	man	True	NaN	Southampton	no	True

Let's filter some of the numeric columns from the dataset, and see if they contain any missing values.

Script 2:

```
titanic_data = titanic_data[["survived", "pclass", "age",
"fare"]]
titanic_data.head()
```

Output:

	survived	pclass	age	fare
0	0	3	22.0	7.2500
1	1	1	38.0	71.2833
2	1	3	26.0	7.9250
3	1	1	35.0	53.1000
4	0	3	35.0	8.0500

To find the missing values from the aforementioned columns, you need to first call the isnull() method on the titanic_ data dataframe, and then you need to call the mean() method as shown below:

Script 3:

```
titanic_data.isnull().mean()
```

Output:

```
survived  0.000000
pclass    0.000000
age       0.198653
fare      0.000000
dtype: float64
```

The output shows that only the *age* column contains missing values. And the ratio of missing values is around 19.86 percent.

Let's now find out the median and mean values for all the non-missing values in the *age* column.

Script 4:

```
median = titanic_data.age.median()
print(median)

mean = titanic_data.age.mean()
print(mean)
```

Output:

```
28.0
29.69911764705882
```

The age column has a median value of 28 and a mean value of 29.6991.

To plot the kernel density plots for the actual age and median and mean age, we will add columns to the Pandas dataframe.

Script 5:

```
import numpy as np

titanic_data['Median_Age'] = titanic_data.age.fillna(median)

titanic_data['Mean_Age'] = titanic_data.age.fillna(mean)

titanic_data['Mean_Age'] = np.round(titanic_data['Mean_Age'],
1)

titanic_data.head(20)
```

The above script adds `Median_Age` and `Mean_Age` columns to the `titanic_data` dataframe and prints the first 20 records. Here is the output of the above script:

Output:

	survived	pclass	age	fare	Median_Age	Mean_Age
0	0	3	22.0	7.2500	22.0	22.0
1	1	1	38.0	71.2833	38.0	38.0
2	1	3	26.0	7.9250	26.0	26.0
3	1	1	35.0	53.1000	35.0	35.0
4	0	3	35.0	8.0500	35.0	35.0
5	0	3	NaN	8.4583	28.0	29.7
6	0	1	54.0	51.8625	54.0	54.0
7	0	3	2.0	21.0750	2.0	2.0
8	1	3	27.0	11.1333	27.0	27.0
9	1	2	14.0	30.0708	14.0	14.0
10	1	3	4.0	16.7000	4.0	4.0
11	1	1	58.0	26.5500	58.0	58.0
12	0	3	20.0	8.0500	20.0	20.0
13	0	3	39.0	31.2750	39.0	39.0
14	0	3	14.0	7.8542	14.0	14.0
15	1	2	55.0	16.0000	55.0	55.0
16	0	3	2.0	29.1250	2.0	2.0
17	1	2	NaN	13.0000	28.0	29.7
18	0	3	31.0	18.0000	31.0	31.0
19	1	3	NaN	7.2250	28.0	29.7

The highlighted rows in the above output show that NaN, i.e., null values in the age column, have been replaced by the median values in the Median_Age column and by mean values in the Mean_Age column.

The mean and median imputation can affect the data distribution for the columns containing the missing values.

Specifically, the variance of the column is decreased by mean and median imputation now since more values are added to the center of the distribution. The following script plots the distribution of data for the age, `Median_Age`, and `Mean_Age` columns.

Script 6:

```
plt.rcParams["figure.figsize"] = [8,6]

fig = plt.figure()
ax = fig.add_subplot(111)

titanic_data['age'] .plot(kind='kde', ax=ax)

titanic_data['Median_Age'] .plot(kind='kde', ax=ax,
color='red')

titanic_data['Mean_Age'] .plot(kind='kde', ax=ax,
color='green')

lines, labels = ax.get_legend_handles_labels()
ax.legend(lines, labels, loc='best')
```

Here is the output of the script above:

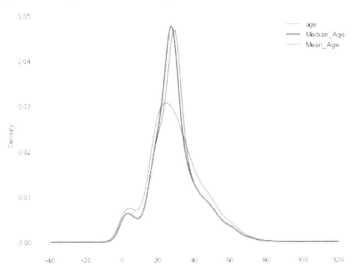

You can clearly see that the default values in the *age* columns have been distorted by the mean and median imputation, and the overall variance of the dataset has also been decreased.

Recommendations

Mean and Median imputation could be used for missing numerical data in case the data is missing at random. If the data is normally distributed, mean imputation is better, or else median imputation is preferred in case of skewed distributions.

Advantages

Mean and median imputations are easy to implement and are a useful strategy to quickly obtain a large dataset. Furthermore, the mean and median imputations can be implemented during the production phase.

Disadvantages

As said earlier, the biggest disadvantage of mean and median imputation is that it affects the default data distribution and variance and covariance of the data.

3.3.2. End of Distribution Imputation

The mean and median imputation and the CCA are not good techniques for missing value imputations in case the data is not randomly missing. For randomly missing data, the most commonly used techniques are end of distribution/ end of tail imputation. In the end of tail imputation, a value is chosen from the tail end of the data. This value signifies that the actual data for the record was missing. Hence, data that is not randomly missing can be taken to account while training statistical models on the data.

In case the data is normally distributed, the end of distribution value can be calculated by multiplying the mean with three standard deviations. In the case of skewed data distributions, the Inter Quartile Rule can be used to find the tail values.

IQR = 75th Quantile – 25th Quantile

Upper IQR Limit = 75th Quantile + IQR x 1.5

Lower IQR Limit = 25th Quantile – IQR x 1.5

Let's perform the end of tail imputation on the age column of the Titanic dataset.

The following script imports the Titanic dataset, filters the numeric columns and then finds the percentage of missing values in each column.

Script 7:

```
import matplotlib.pyplot as plt
import seaborn as sns

plt.rcParams["figure.figsize"] = [8,6]
sns.set_style("darkgrid")

titanic_data = sns.load_dataset('titanic')



titanic_data = titanic_data[["survived", "pclass", "age",
"fare"]]


titanic_data.isnull().mean()
```

Output:

```
survived  0.000000
pclass    0.000000
age       0.198653
fare      0.000000
dtype: float64
```

The above output shows that only the *age* column has missing values, which are around 20 percent of the whole dataset.

The next step is plotting the data distribution for the *age* column. A histogram can reveal the data distribution of a column.

Script 8:

```
titanic_data.age.hist(bins=50)
```

Output:

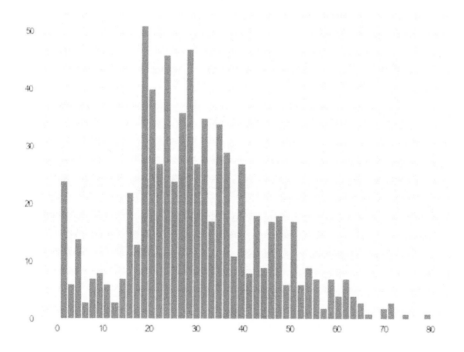

The output shows that the *age* column has an almost normal distribution. Hence, the end of the distribution value can be calculated by multiplying the mean value of the age column by three standard deviations.

The above output again shows that,

Script 9:

```
eod_value = titanic_data.age.mean() + 3 * titanic_data.age.std()
print(eod_value)
```

Output:

73.278

Finally, the missing values in the *age* column can be replaced by the end of tail value calculated in script 9.

Script 10:

```
import numpy as np

titanic_data['age_eod'] = titanic_data.age.fillna(eod_value)
titanic_data.head(20)
```

Output:

	survived	pclass	age	fare	age_eod
0	0	3	22.0	7.2500	22.00000
1	1	1	38.0	71.2833	38.00000
2	1	3	26.0	7.9250	26.00000
3	1	1	35.0	53.1000	35.00000
4	0	3	35.0	8.0500	35.00000
5	0	3	NaN	8.4583	73.27861
6	0	1	54.0	51.8625	54.00000
7	0	3	2.0	21.0750	2.00000
8	1	3	27.0	11.1333	27.00000
9	1	2	14.0	30.0708	14.00000
10	1	3	4.0	16.7000	4.00000
11	1	1	58.0	26.5500	58.00000
12	0	3	20.0	8.0500	20.00000
13	0	3	39.0	31.2750	39.00000
14	0	3	14.0	7.8542	14.00000
15	1	2	55.0	16.0000	55.00000
16	0	3	2.0	29.1250	2.00000
17	1	2	NaN	13.0000	73.27861
18	0	3	31.0	18.0000	31.00000
19	1	3	NaN	7.2250	73.27861

The above output shows that the end of distribution value, i.e., ~73, has replaced the NaN values in the age column.

Finally, you can plot the kernel density estimation plot for the original *age* column and the *age* column with the end of distribution imputation.

Script 11:

```
plt.rcParams["figure.figsize"] = [8,6]

fig = plt.figure()
ax = fig.add_subplot(111)

titanic_data['age'] .plot(kind='kde', ax=ax)
titanic_data['age_eod'] .plot(kind='kde', ax=ax)
lines, labels = ax.get_legend_handles_labels()
ax.legend(lines, labels, loc='best')
```

Output:

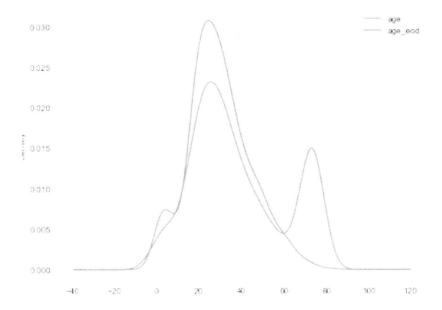

Advantages and Disadvantages

One of the main advantages of the end of distribution imputation is that it can be applied to the dataset where values are not missing at random. The other advantages of end of distribution imputation include its simplicity to understand, ability to create big datasets in a short time, and applicability in the production environment.

The disadvantages include the distortion of data distribution, variance, and covariance.

3.3.3. Arbitrary Value Imputation

In the end of distribution imputation, the values that replace the missing values are calculated from data, while in arbitrary value imputation, the values used to replace missing values are selected arbitrarily.

The arbitrary values are selected in a way that they do not belong to the dataset; rather, they signify the missing values. A good value to select is 99, 999, or any number containing 9s. In case the dataset contains only positive value, a −1 can be chosen as an arbitrary number.

Let's apply the arbitrary value imputation to the age column of the Titanic dataset.

The following script imports the Titanic dataset, filters some of the numeric columns, and displays the percentage of missing values in those columns.

Script 12:

```
import matplotlib.pyplot as plt
import seaborn as sns

plt.rcParams["figure.figsize"] = [8,6]
sns.set_style("darkgrid")

titanic_data = sns.load_dataset('titanic')

titanic_data = titanic_data[["survived", "pclass", "age",
"fare"]]


titanic_data.isnull().mean()
```

Output:

```
survived   0.000000
pclass     0.000000
age        0.198653
fare       0.000000
dtype: float64
```

The output shows that only the *age* column contains some missing values. Next, we plot the histogram for the *age* column to see data distribution.

Script 13:

```
titanic_data.age.hist()
```

Output:

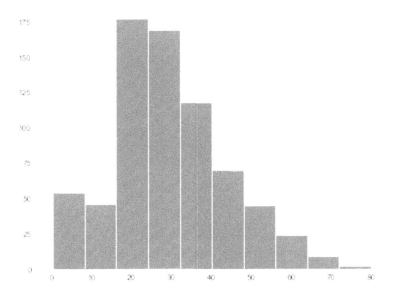

The output shows that the maximum positive value is around 80. Therefore, 99 can be a very good arbitrary value. Furthermore, since the *age* column only contains positive values, −1 can be another very useful arbitrary value. Let's replace the missing values in the age column first by 99, and then by −1.

Script 14:

```
import numpy as np

titanic_data['age_99'] = titanic_data.age.fillna(99)

titanic_data['age_minus1'] = titanic_data.age.fillna(-1)


titanic_data.head(20)
```

Output:

	survived	pclass	age	fare	age_99	age_minus1
0	0	3	22.0	7.2500	22.0	22.0
1	1	1	38.0	71.2833	38.0	38.0
2	1	3	26.0	7.9250	26.0	26.0
3	1	1	35.0	53.1000	35.0	35.0
4	0	3	35.0	8.0500	35.0	35.0
5	0	3	NaN	8.4583	99.0	-1.0
6	0	1	54.0	51.8625	54.0	54.0
7	0	3	2.0	21.0750	2.0	2.0
8	1	3	27.0	11.1333	27.0	27.0
9	1	2	14.0	30.0708	14.0	14.0
10	1	3	4.0	16.7000	4.0	4.0
11	1	1	58.0	26.5500	58.0	58.0
12	0	3	20.0	8.0500	20.0	20.0
13	0	3	39.0	31.2750	39.0	39.0
14	0	3	14.0	7.8542	14.0	14.0
15	1	2	55.0	16.0000	55.0	55.0
16	0	3	2.0	29.1250	2.0	2.0
17	1	2	NaN	13.0000	99.0	-1.0
18	0	3	31.0	18.0000	31.0	31.0
19	1	3	NaN	7.2250	99.0	-1.0

The final step is to plot the kernel density plots for the original *age* column and for the *age* columns where the missing values are replaced by 99 and −1. The following script does that:

Script 15:

```
plt.rcParams["figure.figsize"] = [8,6]

fig = plt.figure()
ax = fig.add_subplot(111)

titanic_data['age'] .plot(kind='kde', ax=ax)

titanic_data['age_99'] .plot(kind='kde', ax=ax, color='red')

titanic_data['age_minus1'] .plot(kind='kde', ax=ax,
color='green')

lines, labels = ax.get_legend_handles_labels()
ax.legend(lines, labels, loc='best')
```

Output:

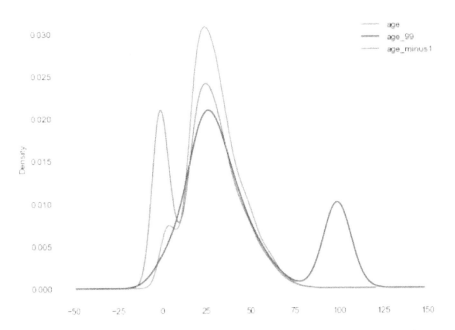

The advantages and disadvantages of arbitrary value imputation are similar to the end of distribution imputation.

It is important to mention that arbitrary value imputation can be used for categorical data as well. In the case of categorical data, you can simply add a value of *missing* in the columns where categorical value is missing.

In this section, we studied the three approaches for handling missing numerical data. In the next section, you will see how to handle missing categorical data.

3.4. Handling Missing Categorical Data

3.4.1. Frequent Category Imputation

One of the most common ways of handling missing values in a categorical column is to replace the missing values with the most frequently occurring values, i.e., the mode of the column. It is for this reason frequent category imputation is also known as mode imputation. Let's see a real-world example of the frequent category imputation.

We will again use the Titanic dataset. We will first try to find the percentage of missing values in the *age, fare,* and *embarked_ town* columns.

Script 16:

```
import matplotlib.pyplot as plt
import seaborn as sns

plt.rcParams["figure.figsize"] = [8,6]
sns.set_style("darkgrid")

titanic_data = sns.load_dataset('titanic')

titanic_data = titanic_data[["embark_town", "age", "fare"]]
titanic_data.head()
titanic_data.isnull().mean()
```

Output:

```
embark_town   0.002245
age         0.198653
fare         0.000000
dtype: float64
```

The output shows that *embark_town* and *age* columns have missing values. The ratio of missing values for the *embark_town* column is very less. Let's plot the bar plot that shows each category in the *embark_town* column against the number of passengers.

Script 17:

```
titanic_data.embark_town.value_counts().sort_
values(ascending=False).plot.bar()
plt.xlabel('Embark Town')
plt.ylabel('Number of Passengers')
```

The output clearly shows that most of the passengers embarked from Southampton.

Output:

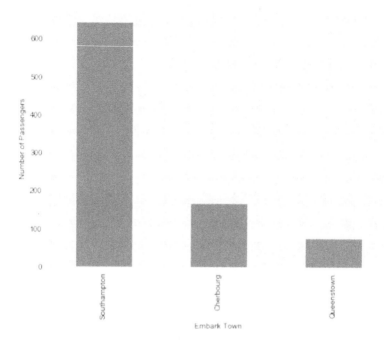

Let's make sure if *Southampton* is actually the mode value for the *embark_town* column.

Script 18:

```
titanic_data.embark_town.mode()
```

Output:

```
0   Southampton
dtype: object
```

Next, we can simply replace the missing values in the *embark town* column by *Southampton*.

Script 19:

```
titanic_data.embark_town.fillna('Southampton',
inplace=True)
```

Let's now find the mode of the *age* column and use it to replace the missing values in the *age* column.

Script 20:

```
titanic_data.age.mode()
```

Output:

24.0

The output shows that the mode of the *age* column is 24. Therefore, we can use this value to replace the missing values in the *age* column.

Script 21:

```
import numpy as np

titanic_data['age_mode'] = titanic_data.age.fillna(24)

titanic_data.head(20)
```

Output:

	embark_town	age	fare	age_mode
0	Southampton	22.0	7.2500	22.0
1	Cherbourg	38.0	71.2833	38.0
2	Southampton	26.0	7.9250	26.0
3	Southampton	35.0	53.1000	35.0
4	Southampton	35.0	8.0500	35.0
5	Queenstown	NaN	8.4583	24.0
6	Southampton	54.0	51.8625	54.0
7	Southampton	2.0	21.0750	2.0
8	Southampton	27.0	11.1333	27.0
9	Cherbourg	14.0	30.0708	14.0
10	Southampton	4.0	16.7000	4.0
11	Southampton	58.0	26.5500	58.0
12	Southampton	20.0	8.0500	20.0
13	Southampton	39.0	31.2750	39.0
14	Southampton	14.0	7.8542	14.0
15	Southampton	55.0	16.0000	55.0
16	Queenstown	2.0	29.1250	2.0
17	Southampton	NaN	13.0000	24.0
18	Southampton	31.0	18.0000	31.0
19	Cherbourg	NaN	7.2250	24.0

Finally, let's plot the kernel density estimation plot for the original *age* column and the *age* column that contains the mode of the values in place of the missing values.

Script 22:

```
plt.rcParams["figure.figsize"] = [8,6]

fig = plt.figure()
ax = fig.add_subplot(111)

titanic_data['age'] .plot(kind='kde', ax=ax)

titanic_data['age_mode'] .plot(kind='kde', ax=ax, color='red')


lines, labels = ax.get_legend_handles_labels()
ax.legend(lines, labels, loc='best')
```

Output:

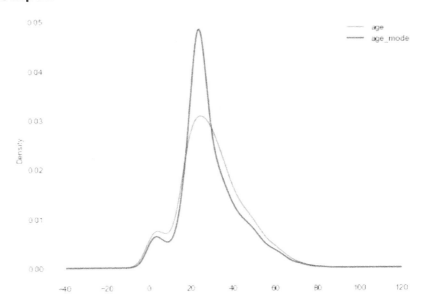

Advantages and Disadvantages

The frequent category imputation is easier to implement on large datasets. Frequent category distribution doesn't make any assumption on the data and can be used in a production environment.

The downside of frequent category imputation is that it can overrepresent the most frequently occurring category in case there are too many missing values in the original dataset. In the case of very small values in the original dataset, the frequent category imputation can result in a new label containing rare values.

3.4.2. Missing Category Imputation

Missing category imputation is similar to arbitrary value imputation. In the case of categorical value, missing value imputation adds an arbitrary category, e.g., *missing* in place of the missing values. Take a look at an example of missing value imputation. Let's load the Titanic dataset and see if any categorical column contains missing values.

Script 23:

```
import matplotlib.pyplot as plt
import seaborn as sns

plt.rcParams["figure.figsize"] = [8,6]
sns.set_style("darkgrid")

titanic_data = sns.load_dataset('titanic')

titanic_data = titanic_data[["embark_town", "age", "fare"]]
titanic_data.head()
titanic_data.isnull().mean()
```

Output:

```
embark_town   0.002245
age           0.198653
fare          0.000000
dtype: float64
```

The output shows that the *embark_town column* is a categorical column that contains some missing values too. We will apply missing value imputation to this column.

Script 24:

```
titanic_data.embark_town.fillna('Missing', inplace=True)
```

After applying missing value imputation, plot the bar plot for the *embark_town* column. You can see that we have a very small, almost negligible plot for the *missing* column.

Script 25:

```
titanic_data.embark_town.value_counts().sort_
values(ascending=False).plot.bar()
plt.xlabel('Embark Town')
plt.ylabel('Number of Passengers')
```

Output:

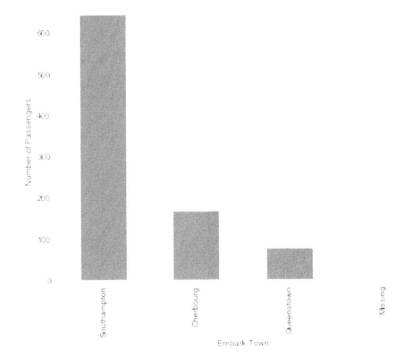

Exercise 3.1

Question 1:

What is the major disadvantage of mean and median imputation?

    A. Distorts the data distribution

    B. Distorts the data variance

    C. Distorts the data covariance

    D. All of the Above

Question 2:

Which imputation should be used when the data is not missing at random?

    A. Mean and Median Imputation

    B. Arbitrary Value Imputation

    C. End of Distribution Imputation

    D. Missing Value Imputation

Question 3:

How should the end of tail distribution be calculated for normal distribution?

A. IQR Rule

B. Mean x 3 Standard deviations

C. Mean

D. Median

Exercise 3.2

Replace the missing values in the *deck* column of the Titanic dataset by the most frequently occurring categories in that column. Plot a bar plot for the updated *deck* column.

Encoding Categorical Data

4.1. Introduction

Models based on statistical algorithms, such as machine learning and deep learning, work with numbers. However, a dataset can contain numerical, categorical, date time, and mixed variables, as you saw in chapter 2. A mechanism is needed to convert categorical data to its numeric counterpart so that the data can be used to build statistical models. The techniques used to convert numeric data into categorical data are called categorical data encoding schemes. In this chapter, you will see some of the most commonly used categorical data encoding schemes.

4.2. One Hot Encoding

One hot encoding is one of the most commonly used categorical encoding schemes. In one hot encoding, for each unique value in a categorical column, a new column is added. Integer 1 is added to the column that corresponds to the original label, and all the remaining columns are filled with zeros. Let's take a look at a very simple example of one hot encoding.

In the following table, we have a categorical column *Country*. The column contains three unique values: USA, UK, and France.

Country	Target
USA	1
UK	0
USA	1
France	1
USA	0
UK	0

The following table contains the one hot encoded version of the above table. In the following table, you can see that three columns have been added, i.e., USA, UK, and FRANCE. In the original column, we had USA as the label in the first row of the *Country* column. In the newly added one hot encoded table, we have 1 in the USA column. Similarly, the original table contained UK as the label in the second row. In the one hot encoded table, we have 1 in the second row for the UK column.

USA	UK	France	Target
1	0	0	1
0	1	0	0
1	0	0	1
0	0	1	1
1	0	0	0
0	1	0	0

As a matter of fact, you only need N-1 columns in the one hot encoded dataset for a column that originally contained N unique labels. Look at the following table:

UK	France	Target
O	O	1
1	O	O
O	O	1
O	1	1
O	O	O
1	O	O

In this table, the USA column has been removed. However, we can still capture the information that the first column contained. For instance, the row where both UK and France columns contain zero actually represents that this record corresponds to the USA column.

Let's see one hot encoding with the help of an example. Execute the following script to download the Titanic dataset, as we did in the previous chapters.

Script 1:

```
import matplotlib.pyplot as plt
import seaborn as sns

plt.rcParams["figure.figsize"] = [8,6]
sns.set_style("darkgrid")

titanic_data = sns.load_dataset('titanic')

titanic_data.head()
```

Output:

	survived	pclass	sex	age	sibsp	parch	fare	embarked	class	who	adult_male	deck	embark_town	alive	alone
0	0	3	male	22.0	1	0	7.2500	S	Third	man	True	NaN	Southampton	no	False
1	1	1	female	38.0	1	0	71.2833	C	First	woman	False	C	Cherbourg	yes	False
2	1	3	female	26.0	0	0	7.9250	S	Third	woman	False	NaN	Southampton	yes	True
3	1	1	female	35.0	1	0	53.1000	S	First	woman	False	C	Southampton	yes	False
4	0	3	male	35.0	0	0	8.0500	S	Third	man	True	NaN	Southampton	no	True

Let's filter the `titanic_data` dataframe by removing all the columns except `sex`, `class`, and `embark_town` columns. These are categorical columns.

Script 2:

```
titanic_data = titanic_data[["sex", "class", "embark_town"]]
titanic_data.head()
```

Output:

	sex	class	embark_town
0	male	Third	Southampton
1	female	First	Cherbourg
2	female	Third	Southampton
3	female	First	Southampton
4	male	Third	Southampton

Let's print the unique values in the three columns in the `titanic_data` dataframe.

Script 3:

```
print(titanic_data['sex'].unique())
print(titanic_data['class'].unique())
print(titanic_data['embark_town'].unique())
```

Output:

```
['male' 'female']
[Third, First, Second]
Categories (3, object): [Third, First, Second]
['Southampton' 'Cherbourg' 'Queenstown' nan]
```

The easiest way to convert a column into one hot-encoded column is by using the `get_dummies()` method of the Pandas dataframe, as shown below:

Script 4:

```
import pandas as pd
temp = pd.get_dummies(titanic_data['sex'])

temp.head()
```

In the output, you will see two columns, one for males and one for females.

Output:

	female	male
0	0	1
1	1	0
2	1	0
3	1	0
4	0	1

Let's display the actual sex name and the one hot encoded version for the sex column in the same dataframe.

Script 5:

```
pd.concat([titanic_data['sex'],
      pd.get_dummies(titanic_data['sex'])], axis=1).head()
```

Output:

	sex	female	male
0	male	0	1
1	female	1	0
2	female	1	0
3	female	1	0
4	male	0	1

From the above output, you can see that in the first row, 1 has been added in the male column because the actual value in the sex column is male. Similarly, in the second row, 1 is added to the female column since the actual value in the sex column is female.

In the same way, we can convert the *embark_town* column into a one hot encoded vector as shown below:

Script 6:

```
import pandas as pd
temp = pd.get_dummies(titanic_data['embark_town'])

temp.head()
```

Output:

	Cherbourg	Queenstown	Southampton
0	0	0	1
1	1	0	0
2	0	0	1
3	0	0	1
4	0	0	1

As you saw earlier, you can have N-1 columns one hot encoded columns for the categorical column that contains N unique labels. You can remove the first column created by get_dummies() method by passing True as the value for drop_first parameter as shown below:

Script 7:

```
import pandas as pd
temp = pd.get_dummies(titanic_data['embark_town'], drop_first =
True)

temp.head()
```

Output:

	Queenstown	Southampton
0	0	1
1	0	0
2	0	1
3	0	1
4	0	1

Also, you can create one hot encoded column for null values in the actual column by passing True as a value for the dummy_na parameter.

Script 8:

```
import pandas as pd
temp = pd.get_dummies(titanic_data['embark_town'], dummy_na =
True ,drop_first = True)

temp.head()
```

Output:

	Queenstown	Southampton	NaN
0	0	1	0
1	0	0	0
2	0	1	0
3	0	1	0
4	0	1	0

The main advantage of one hot encoding is that it makes no assumption about the dataset and all the categorical values can be successfully encoded. A major drawback of this approach is that the feature space can become very large since a categorical column can have a lot of unique values.

4.3. Label Encoding

In label encoding, labels are replaced by integers. This is why label encoding is also called integer encoding. Consider the following table:

Country	Target
USA	1
UK	0
USA	1
France	1
USA	0
UK	0

The above table has been label encoded as follows. You can see that USA has been labeled as 1, UK has been labeled as 2, and France has been labeled as 3.

Country	Target
1	1
2	O
1	1
3	1
1	O
2	O

To implement label encoding, you can use the `LabelEncoder` class from the `sklearn.preprocessing` module, as shown below. You have to create an object of the `label_encoder` class. Next, you need to call the fit() method of the `label_encoder` object and pass it your categorical column. Finally, to convert the categorical column to numerical, call the transform method of the `label_encoder` object, and pass it the categorical column.

The following script performs label encoding on the *class* column of the Titanic dataset.

Script 9:

```
# for integer encoding using sklearn
from sklearn.preprocessing import LabelEncoder

le = LabelEncoder()

le.fit(titanic_data['class'])

titanic_data['le_class'] = le.transform(titanic_data['class'])

titanic_data.head()
```

Output:

	sex	class	embark_town	le_class
0	male	Third	Southampton	2
1	female	First	Cherbourg	0
2	female	Third	Southampton	2
3	female	First	Southampton	0
4	male	Third	Southampton	2

From the above output, you can see that the class Third labeled as 2, the class First is labeled as 0, and so on. It is important to mention that label encoding starts at 0.

4.4. Frequency Encoding

In frequency encoding, each unique label in a categorical column is replaced by its total count or frequency. For instance, in the following table, USA occurs three times, while UK and France have a count of two and one respectively.

Country	Target
USA	1
UK	0
USA	1
France	1
USA	0
UK	0

After frequency encoding, the *Country* column looks like this.

Country	Target
3	1
2	O
3	1
1	1
3	O
2	O

Let's apply frequency encoding on the *embark_town* column of the Titanic dataset. The column contains some null values that can be removed using the following script.

Script 10:

```
titanic_data.dropna(inplace = True)
```

Next, you need to call the value_counts() method on the categorical column, and then chain it with the to_dict() column to obtain the count for each unique label in the actual categorical column as shown below:

Script 11:

```
value_counts = titanic_data['embark_town'].value_counts().
to_dict()
print(value_counts)
```

Output:

```
{'Southampton': 644, 'Cherbourg': 168, 'Queenstown': 77}
```

Finally, call the map() method and pass it the dictionary containing the labels and count.

Script 12:

```
titanic_data['embark_town'] = titanic_data['embark_town'].
map(value_counts)
titanic_data.head()
```

In the output, you can see that the *embark_town* column contains frequencies of actual labels.

Output:

	sex	class	embark_town	le_class
0	male	Third	644	2
1	female	First	168	0
2	female	Third	644	2
3	female	First	644	0
4	male	Third	644	2

You can also add percentage frequency by dividing the label count by the total number of rows as follows:

Script 13:

```
frequency_count = (titanic_data['embark_town'].value_counts()
/ len(titanic_data) ).to_dict()
print(frequency_count)
```

Output:

```
{644: 0.7244094488188977, 168: 0.1889763779527559, 77:
0.08661417322834646}
```

Script 14:

```
titanic_data['embark_town'] = titanic_data['embark_town'].
map(frequency_count)
titanic_data.head()
```

Output:

	sex	class	embark_town	le_class
0	male	Third	0.724409	2
1	female	First	0.188976	0
2	female	Third	0.724409	2
3	female	First	0.724409	0
4	male	Third	0.724409	2

4.5. Ordinal Encoding

In ordinal encoding, the labels are ranked on the basis of their relationship with the target. For instance, in the *Country* column of the table below, you have three rows where the Country is USA for these three rows, and the total sum of the target is 2. Hence, the targeted mean value will be 2/3 = 0.66. For UK, this value is 0 since for both the occurrences of UK, there is a 0 in the *Target* column. Hence, 0/2 = 0. Finally, France will have a value of 1.

Country	Target
USA	1
UK	0
USA	1
France	1
USA	0
UK	0

Next, you rank the labels according to their mean occurrence against the target column. Our rank will be:

France -> 1

USA -> 0.66

UK -> 0

In the ordinal encoded column, the smallest value, i.e., UK will be assigned 0 label, UK will be assigned a label of 1, while France will be assigned 2 as shown below:

Country	Target
1	1
0	0
1	1
2	1
1	0
0	0

Let's apply ordinal encoding on the class column of the Titanic dataset.

Script 15:

```
titanic_data = sns.load_dataset('titanic')
titanic_data = titanic_data[["sex", "class", "embark_town",
"survived"]]

titanic_data.groupby(['class'])['survived'].mean().sort_
values()
```

Output:

```
class
Third    0.242363
Second   0.472826
First    0.629630
Name: survived, dtype: float64
```

You can see that the *First* class has the highest mean value against the *survived* column. You can use any other column as the *target* column. Next, we create a dictionary where class labels are assigned corresponding integer labels. Finally, the map() function is used to create a column that contains ordinal values, as shown below:

Script 16:

```
ordered_cats = titanic_data.groupby(['class'])['survived'].
mean().sort_values().index

cat_map= {k: i for i, k in enumerate(ordered_cats, 0)}

titanic_data['class_ordered'] = titanic_data['class'].map(cat_
map)

titanic_data.head()
```

Output:

	sex	class	embark_town	survived	class_ordered
0	male	Third	Southampton	0	0
1	female	First	Cherbourg	1	2
2	female	Third	Southampton	1	0
3	female	First	Southampton	1	2
4	male	Third	Southampton	0	0

You can see that most passengers survived from the First class, and it has been given the highest label, i.e., 2, and so on.

4.6. Mean Encoding

In mean encoding, the labels are replaced by their mean values with respect to the target labels. For instance, in the *Country* column of the table below, you have three rows where the Country is USA for these three rows, and the total sum of the target is 2. Hence, the targeted mean value will be 2/3 = 0.66. For UK, this value is 0 since for both the occurrences of UK, there is a 0 in the *Target* column. Hence, 0/2 = 0. Finally, France will have a value of 1.

Actual Table:

Country	Target
USA	1
UK	0
USA	1
France	1
USA	0
UK	0

Mean Encoded Table:

Country	Target
0.66	1
0	0
0.66	1
1	1
0.66	0
0	0

The following script applied mean encoding on the `class` column of the Titanic dataset.

Script 17:

```
titanic_data.groupby(['class'])['survived'].mean()
```

Output:

```
class
First    0.629630
Second   0.472826
Third    0.242363
Name: survived, dtype: float64
```

Script 18:

```
mean_labels = titanic_data.groupby(['class'])['survived'].
mean().to_dict()
titanic_data['class_mean'] = titanic_data['class'].map(mean_
labels)
titanic_data.head()
```

Output:

	sex	class	embark_town	survived	class_ordered	class_mean
0	male	Third	Southampton	0	0	0.242363
1	female	First	Cherbourg	1	2	0.629630
2	female	Third	Southampton	1	0	0.242363
3	female	First	Southampton	1	2	0.629630
4	male	Third	Southampton	0	0	0.242363

Hands-on Time – Exercise

Now, it is your turn. Follow the instruction in **the exercise below** to check your understanding of categorical data encoding with Python. The answers to these questions are given at the end of the book.

Exercise 4.1

Question 1:

Which encoding scheme generally leads to the highest number of columns in the encoded dataset?

A. Mean Encoding

B. Ordinal Encoding

C. One Hot Encoding

D. All of the Above

Question 2:

Which attribute is set to True to remove the first column from the one-hot encoded columns generated via the get_dummies() method?

A. drop_first

B. remove_first

C. delete_first

D. None of the above

Question 3:

What is the total number of integer labels in the frequency encoding?

A. One less than the total number of unique labels in the original column

B. Equal to the total number of unique labels in the original column

C. 3

D. None of the above

Exercise 4.2

Apply frequency encoding to the *class* column of the Titanic Dataset:

5

Data Discretization

5.1. Introduction

In the previous chapter, you studied how to perform numerical encoding of the categorical values. In this chapter, you will see how to convert continuous numeric values into discrete intervals.

The process of converting continuous numeric values such as price, age, and weight into discrete intervals is called discretization or binning.

One of the main advantages of discretization is that it can help handle outliers. With discretization, the outliers can be placed into tail intervals along with the remaining inlier values that occur at tails. Discretization is particularly helpful in cases where you have skewed distribution of data.

There are various ways to perform discretization. Discretization can be unsupervised and supervised. In unsupervised discretization, the data is discretized without depending on any particular column in the dataset. On the other hand, in supervised discretization, data is discretized depending upon values in a particular column in the dataset.

In this chapter, you will see some of the most commonly used approaches for discretization.

5.2. Equal Width Discretization

The most common type of discretization approach used is fixed width discretization. In fixed width discretization, the width or the size of all the intervals remains the same. An interval is also called a bin. Equal width discretization is a type of unsupervised discretization technique.

For example, consider a scenario in which you have a column that contains the price of products. The minimum price is 20, whereas the maximum price of a product is 800. If you want to convert the values in the price columns into 10 bins or 10 intervals using equal width discretization, you will simply subtract the lower price value from the maximum price value and will then divide the result by the total number of intervals. In our example, with 10 intervals, the interval length will be 800−20/10 = 78. In the output, you will have 10 intervals where the width of each interval will be 78. The first interval will start from 20 and end at 20+78 = 98, and so on.

Let's now see a practical example of equal width discretization. We will perform equal width discretization on the price column of the Diamonds dataset. The Diamonds dataset comes preloaded with Python's Seaborn library, and therefore, you do not have to download it separately. You only have to have the Seaborn library installed. Execute the following script to load the Diamonds dataset and to display its first five rows.

Script 1:

```
import matplotlib.pyplot as plt
import seaborn as sns
import pandas as pd
import numpy as np
plt.rcParams["figure.figsize"] = [8,6]
sns.set_style("darkgrid")

diamond_data = sns.load_dataset('diamonds')

diamond_data.head()
```

Output:

	carat	cut	color	clarity	depth	table	price	x	y	z
0	0.23	Ideal	E	SI2	61.5	55.0	326	3.95	3.98	2.43
1	0.21	Premium	E	SI1	59.8	61.0	326	3.89	3.84	2.31
2	0.23	Good	E	VS1	56.9	65.0	327	4.05	4.07	2.31
3	0.29	Premium	I	VS2	62.4	58.0	334	4.20	4.23	2.63
4	0.31	Good	J	SI2	63.3	58.0	335	4.34	4.35	2.75

The output shows that the dataset contains 10 columns. We will only perform discretization on the *price* column. Let's first plot a histogram for the *price* column.

Script 2:

```
sns.distplot(diamond_data['price'])
```

Output:

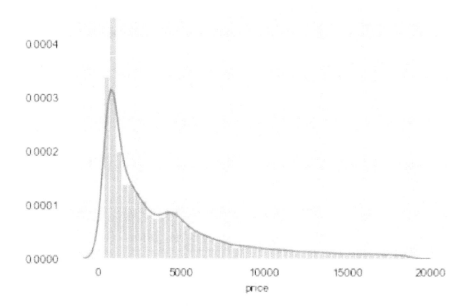

The histogram for the price column shows that our dataset is positively skewed. We can use discretization on this type of data distribution.

Let's now find the total price range by subtracting the minimum price from the maximum price.

Script 3:

```
price_range = diamond_data['price'].max() - diamond_
data['price'].min()
print(price_range )
```

Output:

```
18497
```

The price range is 18497. We will create 10 equal width intervals. To find the length or width of each interval, we simply need to divide the price by the number of intervals.

Script 4:

```
price_range / 10
```

Output:

```
1849.7
```

The output shows the interval length for each of the 10 intervals.

The minimum price will be rounded off to floor, while the maximum price will be rounded off to ceil. The price will be rounded off to the nearest integer value. The following script does that:

Script 5:

```
lower_interval = int(np.floor( diamond_data['price'].min()))
upper_interval = int(np.ceil( diamond_data['price'].max()))


interval_length = int(np.round(price_range / 10))

print(lower_interval)
print(upper_interval)
print(interval_length)
```

Output:

```
326
18823
1850
```

Next, let's create the 10 bins for our dataset. To create bins, we will start with the minimum value, and add the bin interval or length to it. To get the second interval, the interval length will be added to the upper boundary of the first interval and so on. The following script creates 10 equal width bins.

Script 6:

```
total_bins = [i for i in range(lower_interval, upper_
interval+interval_length, interval_length)]
print(total_bins)
```

The following output shows the boundary for each bin.

Output:

```
[326, 2176, 4026, 5876, 7726, 9576, 11426, 13276, 15126,
16976, 18826]
```

Next, we will create string labels for each bin. You can give any name to the bin labels.

Script 7:

```
bin_labels = ['Bin_no_' + str(i) for i in range(1, len(total_
bins))]
print(bin_labels)
```

Output:

```
['Bin_no_1', 'Bin_no_2', 'Bin_no_3', 'Bin_no_4', 'Bin_no_5',
'Bin_no_6', 'Bin_no_7', 'Bin_no_8', 'Bin_no_9', 'Bin_no_10']
```

The output shows the bin labels for our dataset.

You can create the Pandas libraries "cut()" method to convert the continuous column values to numeric bin values. You need to pass the data column that you want to be discretized, along with the bin intervals and the bin labels, as shown below.

Script 8:

```
diamond_data['price_bins'] = pd.cut(x=diamond_data['price'],
bins=total_bins, labels=bin_labels, include_lowest=True)
diamond_data.head(10)
```

Output:

	carat	cut	color	clarity	depth	table	price	x	y	z	price_bins
0	0.23	Ideal	E	SI2	61.5	55.0	326	3.95	3.98	2.43	Bin_no_1
1	0.21	Premium	E	SI1	59.8	61.0	326	3.89	3.84	2.31	Bin_no_1
2	0.23	Good	E	VS1	56.9	65.0	327	4.05	4.07	2.31	Bin_no_1
3	0.29	Premium	I	VS2	62.4	58.0	334	4.20	4.23	2.63	Bin_no_1
4	0.31	Good	J	SI2	63.3	58.0	335	4.34	4.35	2.75	Bin_no_1
5	0.24	Very Good	J	VVS2	62.8	57.0	336	3.94	3.96	2.48	Bin_no_1
6	0.24	Very Good	I	VVS1	62.3	57.0	336	3.95	3.98	2.47	Bin_no_1
7	0.26	Very Good	H	SI1	61.9	55.0	337	4.07	4.11	2.53	Bin_no_1
8	0.22	Fair	E	VS2	65.1	61.0	337	3.87	3.78	2.49	Bin_no_1
9	0.23	Very Good	H	VS1	59.4	61.0	338	4.00	4.05	2.39	Bin_no_1

In the above output, you can see that a column *price_bins* has been added that shows the bin value for the price.

Next, let's plot a bar plot that shows the frequency of prices in each bin.

Script 9:

```
diamond_data.groupby('price_bins')['price'].count().plot.bar()
plt.xticks(rotation=45)
```

Output:

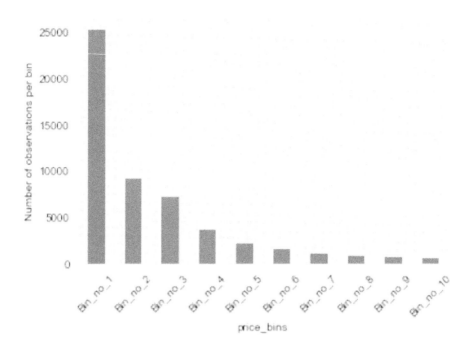

The output shows that the price of most of the diamonds lies in the first bin or the first interval.

5.3. Equal Frequency Discretization

In equal frequency discretization, the bin width is adjusted automatically in such a way that each bin contains exactly the same number of records or has the same frequency. Hence, the name equal frequency discretization. In equal frequency discretization, the bin interval may not be the same. Equal frequency discretization, like equal width discretization, is a supervised discretization technique.

Let's apply equal frequency discretization on the *price* column of the Diamonds dataset as we did previously and see what bins we get.

The following script downloads the Diamonds dataset.

Script 10:

```
import matplotlib.pyplot as plt
import seaborn as sns
import pandas as pd
import numpy as np
plt.rcParams["figure.figsize"] = [8,6]
sns.set_style("darkgrid")

diamond_data = sns.load_dataset('diamonds')

diamond_data.head()
```

Output:

	carat	cut	color	clarity	depth	table	price	x	y	z
0	0.23	Ideal	E	SI2	61.5	55.0	326	3.95	3.98	2.43
1	0.21	Premium	E	SI1	59.8	61.0	326	3.89	3.84	2.31
2	0.23	Good	E	VS1	56.9	65.0	327	4.05	4.07	2.31
3	0.29	Premium	I	VS2	62.4	58.0	334	4.20	4.23	2.63
4	0.31	Good	J	SI2	63.3	58.0	335	4.34	4.35	2.75

To convert a continuous column into equal frequency discretized bins, you can use the "qcut()" function. The function returns quartiles, equal to the number of specified intervals along with the bins. You have to pass the dataset column, the number of intervals, the labels as mandatory parameters for the "qcut()" function. The following script returns equal frequency 10 bins for the price column of the Diamonds dataset. Next, we create a dataframe that shows the actual price and quartile information.

Script 11:

```
discretised_price, bins = pd.qcut(diamond_data['price'], 10,
labels=None, retbins=True, precision=3, duplicates='raise')

pd.concat([discretised_price, diamond_data['price']], axis=1).
head(10)
```

Output:

	price	price
0	(325.999, 646.0]	326
1	(325.999, 646.0]	326
2	(325.999, 646.0]	327
3	(325.999, 646.0]	334
4	(325.999, 646.0]	335
5	(325.999, 646.0]	336
6	(325.999, 646.0]	336
7	(325.999, 646.0]	337
8	(325.999, 646.0]	337
9	(325.999, 646.0]	338

To see the bin intervals, simply print the *bins* returned by the "qcut()" function as shown below:

Script 12:

```
print(bins)
print(type(bins))
```

Output:

```
[ 326.  646.  837.  1087.  1698.  2401.  3465.  4662.  6301.2
 9821. 18823. ]
<class 'numpy.ndarray'>
```

Next, let's find the number of records per bin. Execute the following script:

Script 13:

```
discretised_price.value_counts()
```

Output:

```
(325.999, 646.0]     5411
(1698.0, 2401.0]     5405
(837.0, 1087.0]    5396
(6301.2, 9821.0]    5395
(3465.0, 4662.0]    5394
(9821.0, 18823.0]   5393
(4662.0, 6301.2]    5389
(1087.0, 1698.0]    5388
(646.0, 837.0]     5385
(2401.0, 3465.0]    5384
Name: price, dtype: int64
```

From the output, you can see that all the bins have more or less the same number of records. This is what equal frequency discretization does, i.e., create bins with an equal number of records.

Next, to create a Pandas dataframe containing the bins, we first create 10 labels since we created 10 bins.

Script 14:

```
bin_labels = ['Bin_no_' +str(i) for i in range(1,11)]
print(bin_labels)
```

Output:

```
['Bin_no_1', 'Bin_no_2', 'Bin_no_3', 'Bin_no_4', 'Bin_no_5',
 'Bin_no_6', 'Bin_no_7', 'Bin_no_8', 'Bin_no_9', 'Bin_no_10']
```

To perform binning, we can again use the Pandas library's "cut()" method as shown below:

Script 15:

```
diamond_data['price_bins'] = pd.cut(x=diamond_data['price'],
bins=bins, labels=bin_labels, include_lowest=True)
diamond_data.head(10)
```

Output:

	carat	cut	color	clarity	depth	table	price	x	y	z	price_bins
0	0.23	Ideal	E	SI2	61.5	55.0	326	3.95	3.98	2.43	Bin_no_1
1	0.21	Premium	E	SI1	59.8	61.0	326	3.89	3.84	2.31	Bin_no_1
2	0.23	Good	E	VS1	56.9	65.0	327	4.05	4.07	2.31	Bin_no_1
3	0.29	Premium	I	VS2	62.4	58.0	334	4.20	4.23	2.63	Bin_no_1
4	0.31	Good	J	SI2	63.3	58.0	335	4.34	4.35	2.75	Bin_no_1
5	0.24	Very Good	J	VVS2	62.8	57.0	336	3.94	3.96	2.48	Bin_no_1
6	0.24	Very Good	I	VVS1	62.3	57.0	336	3.95	3.98	2.47	Bin_no_1
7	0.26	Very Good	H	SI1	61.9	55.0	337	4.07	4.11	2.53	Bin_no_1
8	0.22	Fair	E	VS2	65.1	61.0	337	3.87	3.78	2.49	Bin_no_1
9	0.23	Very Good	H	VS1	59.4	61.0	338	4.00	4.05	2.39	Bin_no_1

In the output above, you can see a new column, i.e., *price_bins*. This column contains equal frequency discrete bin labels. Finally, we can plot a bar plot that displays the frequency of records per bin.

Script 16:

```
diamond_data.groupby('price_bins')['price'].count().plot.bar()
plt.xticks(rotation=45)
```

Output:

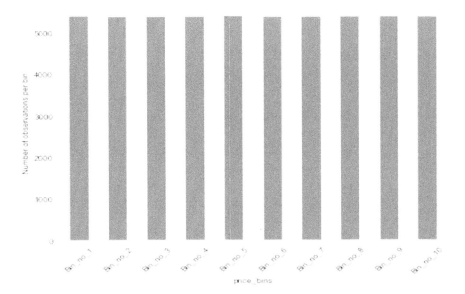

You can see that the number of records is almost the same for all the bins.

5.4. K-Means Discretization

K-means discretization is another unsupervised discretization technique based on the K-means algorithm. A brief description of the K-Means algorithm is given below:

1. In the beginning, K random clusters of data points are created, where K is the number of bins or intervals.

2. Each data point is linked to the closest cluster center.

3. The centers of all the clusters are updated based on the associated data points.

Let's use K-Means discretization to discretize the *price* column of the Diamonds dataset. The following script imports the dataset.

Script 17:

```
import matplotlib.pyplot as plt
import seaborn as sns
import pandas as pd
import numpy as np
from sklearn.preprocessing import KBinsDiscretizer

plt.rcParams["figure.figsize"] = [8,6]
sns.set_style("darkgrid")

diamond_data = sns.load_dataset('diamonds')

diamond_data.head()
```

Output:

	carat	cut	color	clarity	depth	table	price	x	y	z
0	0.23	Ideal	E	SI2	61.5	55.0	326	3.95	3.98	2.43
1	0.21	Premium	E	SI1	59.8	61.0	326	3.89	3.84	2.31
2	0.23	Good	E	VS1	56.9	65.0	327	4.05	4.07	2.31
3	0.29	Premium	I	VS2	62.4	58.0	334	4.20	4.23	2.63
4	0.31	Good	J	SI2	63.3	58.0	335	4.34	4.35	2.75

Next, to perform discretization, you need to call the **"KBinsDiscretizer()"** method and pass it the number of bins. On the object returned by the **"KBinsDiscretizer()"** method, you need to call the **"fit()"** method and pass it the price column, as shown below:

Script 18:

```
discretization = KBinsDiscretizer(n_bins=10, encode='ordinal',
strategy='kmeans')

discretization.fit(diamond_data[['price']])
```

Next, you can access the bins created via K-means clustering using the "`bin_edges`" attribute.

Script 19:

```
intervals = discretization.bin_edges_.tolist()
print(intervals)
```

Output:

```
[array([ 326.    , 1417.67543928, 2627.50524806, 3950.3762392,
    5441.70606939, 7160.05893161, 9140.61465361,
11308.37609661,
    13634.55462656, 16130.22549621, 18823.    ])]
```

Let's create a list of the bins created via K-means discretization.

Script 20:

```
intervals = [ 326.    , 1417.67543928, 2627.50524806,
3950.3762392 ,
    5441.70606939, 7160.05893161, 9140.61465361,
11308.37609661,
    13634.55462656, 16130.22549621, 18823.    ]
```

The following script creates a list of labels for each bin.

Script 21:

```
bin_labels = ['Bin_no_' +str(i) for i in range(1,11)]
print(bin_labels)
```

Output:

```
['Bin_no_1', 'Bin_no_2', 'Bin_no_3', 'Bin_no_4', 'Bin_
no_5', 'Bin_no_6', 'Bin_no_7', 'Bin_no_8', 'Bin_no_9',
'Bin_no_10']
```

Finally, you can use the *cut* method of the P*andas* dataframe to create a new column containing bins for the *price* column.

Script 22:

```
diamond_data['price_bins'] = pd.cut(x=diamond_data['price'],
bins=intervals, labels=bin_labels, include_lowest=True)
diamond_data.head(10)
```

Output:

	carat	cut	color	clarity	depth	table	price	x	y	z	price_bins
0	0.23	Ideal	E	SI2	61.5	55.0	326	3.95	3.98	2.43	Bin_no_1
1	0.21	Premium	E	SI1	59.8	61.0	326	3.89	3.84	2.31	Bin_no_1
2	0.23	Good	E	VS1	56.9	65.0	327	4.05	4.07	2.31	Bin_no_1
3	0.29	Premium	I	VS2	62.4	58.0	334	4.20	4.23	2.63	Bin_no_1
4	0.31	Good	J	SI2	63.3	58.0	335	4.34	4.35	2.75	Bin_no_1
5	0.24	Very Good	J	VVS2	62.8	57.0	336	3.94	3.96	2.48	Bin_no_1
6	0.24	Very Good	I	VVS1	62.3	57.0	336	3.95	3.98	2.47	Bin_no_1
7	0.26	Very Good	H	SI1	61.9	55.0	337	4.07	4.11	2.53	Bin_no_1
8	0.22	Fair	E	VS2	65.1	61.0	337	3.87	3.78	2.49	Bin_no_1
9	0.23	Very Good	H	VS1	59.4	61.0	338	4.00	4.05	2.39	Bin_no_1

The following script plots a bar plot displaying the frequencies of records per bin.

Script 23:

```
diamond_data.groupby('price_bins')['price'].count().plot.bar()
plt.xticks(rotation=45)
```

Output:

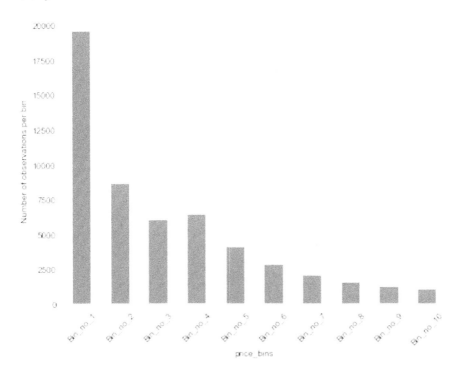

5.5. Decision Tree Discretization

Decision tree discretization is a type of supervised discretization algorithm. In decision tree discretization, bins are created based on the values in some other columns. Let's download the Diamonds dataset first.

Script 24:

```
import matplotlib.pyplot as plt
import seaborn as sns
import pandas as pd
import numpy as np
from sklearn.preprocessing import KBinsDiscretizer
from sklearn.tree import DecisionTreeClassifier


sns.set_style("darkgrid")


diamond_data = sns.load_dataset('diamonds')


diamond_data.head()
```

Output:

	carat	cut	color	clarity	depth	table	price	x	y	z
0	0.23	Ideal	E	SI2	61.5	55.0	326	3.95	3.98	2.43
1	0.21	Premium	E	SI1	59.8	61.0	326	3.89	3.84	2.31
2	0.23	Good	E	VS1	56.9	65.0	327	4.05	4.07	2.31
3	0.29	Premium	I	VS2	62.4	58.0	334	4.20	4.23	2.63
4	0.31	Good	J	SI2	63.3	58.0	335	4.34	4.35	2.75

In decision tree discretization, we do not specify the number of bins or intervals. Rather, the decision tree identifies the optimal number of bins.

To implement decision tree discretization, you can use the **"DecisionTreeClassifier"** class from the **"sklearn.tree"** module. You need to call the **"fit()"** method on the class and pass the continuous column name and the column on the basis of which you want to create your bins.

For instance, the following script creates bins for the *price* column of the Diamonds dataset, based on the values in the *cut* column.

Script 25:

```
tree_model = DecisionTreeClassifier(max_depth=3)

tree_model.fit(diamond_data['price'].to_frame(), diamond_
data['cut'])

diamond_data['price_tree']= tree_model.predict_proba(diamond_
data['price'].to_frame())[:,1]

diamond_data.head()
```

Output:

	carat	cut	color	clarity	depth	table	price	x	y	z	price_tree
0	0.23	Ideal	E	SI2	61.5	55.0	326	3.95	3.98	2.43	0.127435
1	0.21	Premium	E	SI1	59.8	61.0	326	3.89	3.84	2.31	0.127435
2	0.23	Good	E	VS1	56.9	65.0	327	4.05	4.07	2.31	0.127435
3	0.29	Premium	I	VS2	62.4	58.0	334	4.20	4.23	2.63	0.127435
4	0.31	Good	J	SI2	63.3	58.0	335	4.34	4.35	2.75	0.127435

You can find the unique probability values in the *price_tree* column using the following script:

Script 26:

```
diamond_data['price_tree'].unique()
```

Output:

```
array([0.12743549, 0.10543414, 0.0964318 , 0.11666667,
0.15124195,
    0.08576481, 0.05252665, 0.08874839])
```

The following script plots the frequency of records per bin.

Script 27:

```
diamond_data.groupby(['price_tree'])['price'].count().plot.
bar()
plt.xticks(rotation=45)
```

Output:

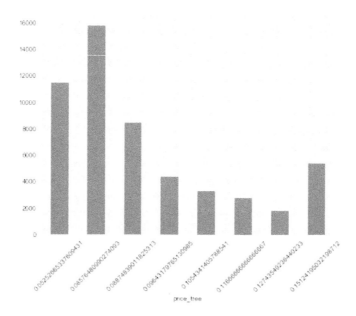

5.6. Custom Discretization

Finally, you can perform customized discretization of a continuous column by passing custom bin values. Let's discretize the *tip* column of the Tips dataset. The following script downloads the Tips dataset.

Script 28:

```
import matplotlib.pyplot as plt
import seaborn as sns
import pandas as pd
import numpy as np
from sklearn.preprocessing import KBinsDiscretizer
from sklearn.tree import DecisionTreeClassifier

sns.set_style("darkgrid")

tips_data = sns.load_dataset('tips')

tips_data.head()
```

Output:

	total_bill	tip	sex	smoker	day	time	size
0	16.99	1.01	Female	No	Sun	Dinner	2
1	10.34	1.66	Male	No	Sun	Dinner	3
2	21.01	3.50	Male	No	Sun	Dinner	3
3	23.68	3.31	Male	No	Sun	Dinner	2
4	24.59	3.61	Female	No	Sun	Dinner	4

Let's find the maximum and minimum values in the *tip* column.

Script 29:

```
tips_data['tip'].describe()
```

Output:

```
count   244.000000
mean      2.998279
std       1.383638
min       1.000000
25%       2.000000
50%       2.900000
75%       3.562500
max      10.000000
Name: tip, dtype: float64
```

You can see that the *tip* column has a minimum value of 1 and a maximum value of 10. We will create three bins for the *tip* column. The first bin will contain records where the tip is between 0 and 3. The second bin will contain records where the tip is between 3 and 7, and finally, the third bin will contain records between 7 and 10. After that, you can simply use the "cut()" method from the Pandas library to create a column that contains customized bins, as shown in the following script:

Script 30:

```
buckets = [0, 3, 7, 10]


labels = ['0-3', '3-7', '7-10']


tips_data['tip_bins'] = pd.cut(tips_data['tip'], bins=buckets,
labels=labels, include_lowest=True)

tips_data.head()
```

Output:

	total_bill	tip	sex	smoker	day	time	size	tip_bins
0	16.99	1.01	Female	No	Sun	Dinner	2	0-3
1	10.34	1.66	Male	No	Sun	Dinner	3	0-3
2	21.01	3.50	Male	No	Sun	Dinner	3	3-7
3	23.68	3.31	Male	No	Sun	Dinner	2	3-7
4	24.59	3.61	Female	No	Sun	Dinner	4	3-7

Finally, the number of records per bin can be plotted via a bar plot.

Script 31:

```
tips_data.groupby('tip_bins')['tip'].count().plot.bar()
plt.xticks(rotation=45)
```

Output:

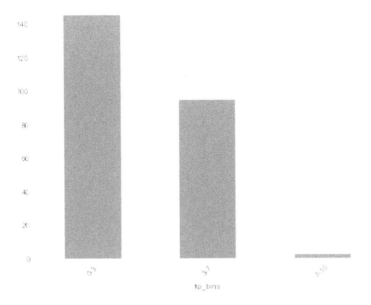

Exercise 5.1

Question 1:

Which of the following discretization scheme is supervised?

    A. K Means Discretization

    B. Decision Tree Discretization

    C. Equal Width Discretization

    D. Equal Frequency Discretization

Question 2:

Which of the following discretization scheme generates bins of equal sizes?

    A. K Means Discretization

    B. Decision Tree Discretization

    C. Equal Frequency Discretization

    D. None of the Above

Question 3:

Which of the following discretization scheme generates bins containing an equal number of samples?

    A. K Means Discretization

    B. Decision Tree Discretization

    C. Equal Frequency Discretization

    D. Equal Width Distribution

Exercise 5.2

Create five bins for the *total_bill* column of the Tips dataset using equal frequency discretization. Plot a bar plot displaying the frequency of bills per category.

6

Outlier Handling

6.1. Introduction

Outliers have been briefly explained in section 9 of chapter 2. In that section, you studied what the different types of outliers are, how they occur in a dataset, and how they can affect the performance of statistical machine learning and deep learning models. In this chapter, you are going to see how to handle outliers.

There are four main techniques to handle outliers:

1. You can totally remove the outliers from the dataset.

2. You can treat outliers as missing values, and then apply any data imputation technique that you studied in chapter 3.

3. You can apply discretization techniques to the dataset that will include the outlier along with other data points at the tail.

4. You can cap or censor the outliers and replace them with maximum and minimum values that can be found via several techniques.

You have already studied discretization and missing value imputation in the previous chapters. In this chapter, we will focus on trimming and capping.

6.2. Outlier Trimming

Outlier trimming, as the name suggests, refers to simply removing the outliers beyond a certain threshold value. One of the main advantages of outlier trimming is it is extremely quick and doesn't distort the data. A downside to outlier trimming is it can reduce the data size.

There are several ways to find the thresholds for outlier trimming.

Let's remove the outliers from the *age* column of the Titanic dataset. The Titanic dataset contains records of the passengers who traveled on the unfortunate *Titanic* that sank in 1912. The following script imports the Titanic dataset from the Seaborn library.

Script 1:

```
import matplotlib.pyplot as plt
import seaborn as sns
import pandas as pd
import numpy as np

plt.rcParams["figure.figsize"] = [8,6]
sns.set_style("darkgrid")

titanic_data = sns.load_dataset('titanic')

titanic_data.head()
```

The first five rows of the Titanic dataset look like this.

Output:

survived	pclass	sex	age	sibsp	parch	fare	embarked	class	who	adult_male	deck	embark_town	alive	alone
0	0	3	male	22 0	1	0	7 2500	S	Third	man	True	NaN	Southampton	no	False
1	1	1	female	38 0	1	0	71 2833	C	First	woman	False	C	Cherbourg	yes	False
2	1	3	female	26 0	0	0	7 9250	S	Third	woman	False	NaN	Southampton	yes	True
3	1	1	female	35 0	1	0	53 1000	S	First	woman	False	C	Southampton	yes	False
4	0	3	male	35 0	0	0	8 0500	S	Third	man	True	NaN	Southampton	no	True

To visualize the outliers, you can simply plot the box plot for the *age* column, as shown below:

Script 2:

```
sns.boxplot( y='age', data=titanic_data)
```

Output:

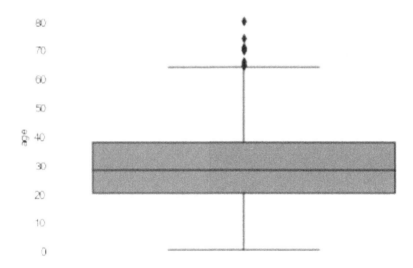

You can see that there are a few outliers in the form of black dots at the upper end of the age distribution in the box plot.

To remove a quartile, we first need to define the values that will be considered as quartiles. There are various ways to do so. One of the most common ways to do this is to find the Inter Quartile Range (IQR), multiply it by 1.5, and then subtract it from the first quartile value (0.25 quantile) to find the lower limit. To find the upper limit, add the product of IQR and 1.5 to the 3rd quartile value (0.75 quantile). IQR can be calculated by subtracting the first quartile value from the 4th quartile.

The following script finds the lower and upper limits for the outliers for the *age* column.

Script 3:

```
IQR = titanic_data["age"].quantile(0.75) - titanic_
data["age"].quantile(0.25)

lower_age_limit = titanic_data["age"].quantile(0.25) - (IQR *
1.5)
upper_age_limit = titanic_data["age"].quantile(0.75) + (IQR *
1.5)

print(lower_age_limit)
print(upper_age_limit)
```

Output:

```
-6.6875
64.8125
```

The output shows that any age value larger than 64.81 and smaller than -6.68 will be considered an outlier. The following script finds the rows containing the outlier values:

Script 4:

```
age_outliers = np.where(titanic_data["age"] > upper_age_limit,
True,
           np.where(titanic_data["age"] < lower_age_limit,
True, False))
```

Finally, the following script removes the rows containing the outlier values from the actual Titanic dataset.

Script 5:

```
titanic_without_age_outliers = titanic_data.loc[~(age_
outliers), ]

titanic_data.shape, titanic_without_age_outliers.shape
```

The output shows the number of records before and after removing the outliers.

Output:

```
((891, 15), (880, 15))
```

Finally, you can plot a box plot to see if the outliers have actually been removed.

Script 6:

```
sns.boxplot( y='age', data = titanic_without_age_outliers)
```

Output:

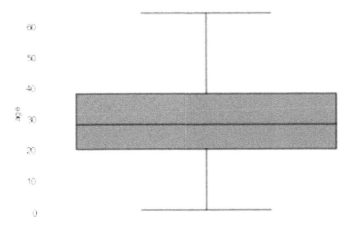

You can see from the above output that the dataset doesn't contain any outliers now.

6.3. Outlier Capping Using IQR

In outlier trimming, the outliers are removed from the dataset. In outlier capping, the outliers are capped at certain minimum and maximum values. The rows containing the outliers are not removed from the dataset. We will again use the Inter Quartile Range technique to find the lower and upper limit for the outliers in the *fare* column of the Titanic dataset. The following script imports the Titanic dataset.

Script 7:

```
import matplotlib.pyplot as plt
import seaborn as sns
import pandas as pd
import numpy as np

plt.rcParams["figure.figsize"] = [8,6]
sns.set_style("darkgrid")

titanic_data = sns.load_dataset('titanic')
```

The following script plots a box plot for the *fare* column of the Titanic dataset.

Script 8:

```
sns.boxplot( y='fare', data=titanic_data)
```

Output:

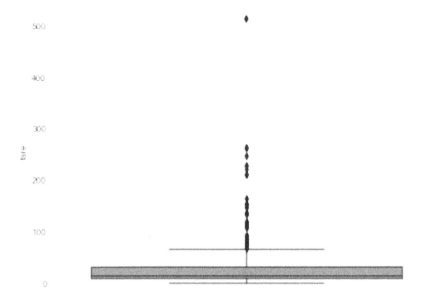

You can see that the *fare* column has a very high variance owing to the presence of a large number of outliers. Let's plot a distribution plot to see the histogram distribution of data in the *fare* column.

Script 9:

```
sns.distplot(titanic_data['fare'])
```

The output shows that the data in the *fare* column is positively skewed.

Output:

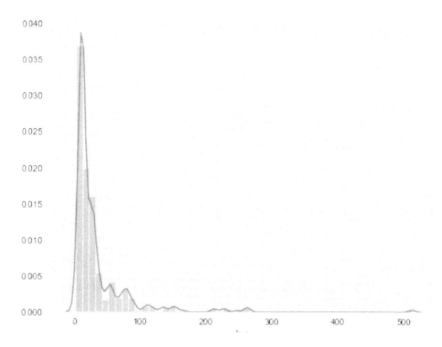

We will again use the IQR method to find the upper and lower limits to find the outliers in the *fare* column.

Script 10:

```
IQR = titanic_data["fare"].quantile(0.75) - titanic_
data["fare"].quantile(0.25)

lower_fare_limit = titanic_data["fare"].quantile(0.25) - (IQR
* 1.5)
upper_fare_limit = titanic_data["fare"].quantile(0.75) + (IQR
* 1.5)

print(lower_fare_limit)
print(upper_fare_limit)
```

The output shows that any fare greater than 65.63 and less than -26.72 is an outlier.

Output:

```
-26.724
65.6344
```

The following script replaces the outlier values by the upper and lower limits. The fare values greater than the upper limit are replaced by the upper limit, and the fare values smaller than the lower limit are replaced by the lower limit. The total number of records in the dataset before and after removing the outliers remains the same.

Script 11:

```
titanic_data["fare"]= np.where(titanic_data["fare"] > upper_
fare_limit, upper_fare_limit,
          np.where(titanic_data["fare"] < lower_fare_limit,
lower_fare_limit, titanic_data["fare"]))
```

Let's now plot a box plot to see if we still have any outliers in the *fare* column.

Script 12:

```
sns.boxplot( y='fare', data=titanic_data)
```

Output:

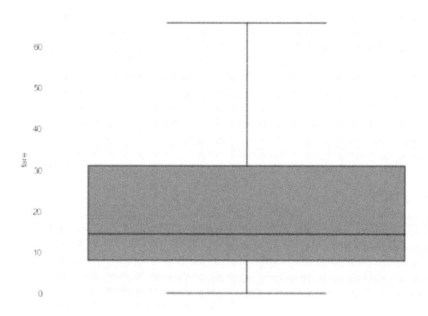

The output shows that all the outliers have been removed.

6.4. Outlier Capping Using Mean and Std

Instead of using the IQR method, the upper and lower thresholds for outliers can be calculated via the mean and standard deviation method. To find the upper threshold, the mean of the data is added to three times the standard deviation value. Similarly, to find the lower threshold, you have to multiply the standard deviation by 3, and then remove the result from the mean.

The following script imports the Titanic dataset.

Script 13:

```
import matplotlib.pyplot as plt
import seaborn as sns
import pandas as pd
import numpy as np

plt.rcParams["figure.figsize"] = [8,6]
sns.set_style("darkgrid")

titanic_data = sns.load_dataset('titanic')
```

Let's plot a box plot that displays the distribution of data in the *Age* column of the Titanic dataset.

Script 14:

```
sns.boxplot( y='age', data=titanic_data)
```

Output:

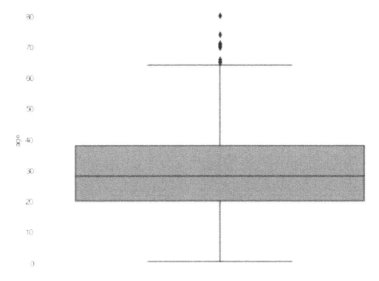

The following script finds the upper and lower Thresholds for the *age* column of the Titanic dataset using the mean and standard deviation capping.

Script 15:

```
lower_age_limit = titanic_data["age"].mean() - (3 * titanic_
data["age"].std())
upper_age_limit = titanic_data["age"].mean() + (3 * titanic_
data["age"].std())

print(lower_age_limit)
print(upper_age_limit)
```

Output:

```
-13.88037434994331
73.27860964406095
```

The output shows that the upper threshold value obtained via the mean and standard deviation capping is 73.27, and the lower limit or threshold is -13.88.

The following script replaces the outlier values by the upper and lower limits.

Script 16:

```
titanic_data["age"]= np.where(titanic_data["age"] > upper_age_
limit, upper_age_limit,
            np.where(titanic_data["age"] < lower_age_limit,
lower_age_limit, titanic_data["age"]))
```

Script 17:

```
sns.boxplot( y='age', data=titanic_data)
```

The box plot shows that we still have some outlier values after applying the mean and standard deviation capping on the *age* column of the Titanic dataset.

Output:

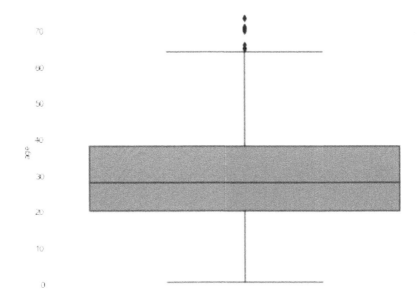

6.5. Outlier Capping Using Quantiles

You can also use quantile information to set the lower and upper limits to find outliers. For instance, we can set 0.05 as the lower limit and 0.95 as the upper limit to find the outliers, which means that if the data point is within the first 5 percent lower values or 5 percent highest values, we consider it as an outlier.

The following script imports the Titanic dataset.

Script 18:

```
import matplotlib.pyplot as plt
import seaborn as sns
import pandas as pd
import numpy as np

plt.rcParams["figure.figsize"] = [8,6]
sns.set_style("darkgrid")

titanic_data = sns.load_dataset('titanic')
```

The following script plots a box plot for the *fare* column of the Titanic dataset.

Script 19:

```
sns.boxplot( y='fare', data=titanic_data)
```

Output:

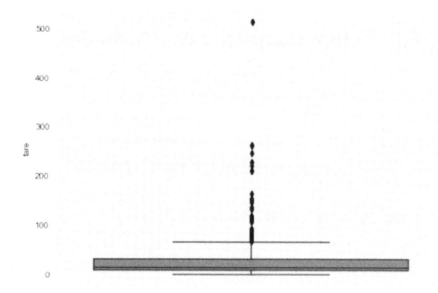

The following script sets 0.05 as the lower limit and 0.95 as the upper limit for the quantiles to find the outliers:

Script 20:

```
lower_fare_limit = titanic_data["fare"].quantile(0.05)
upper_fare_limit = titanic_data["fare"].quantile(0.95)

print(lower_fare_limit)
print(upper_fare_limit)
```

Output:

```
7.225
112.07915
```

The output shows that anything beyond 112.07 is an outlier, and similarly, the *fare* value below 7.22 is also an outlier. The following script replaces the outlier values by the upper and lower limit.

Script 21:

```
titanic_data["fare"]= np.where(titanic_data["fare"] > upper_
fare_limit, upper_fare_limit,
           np.where(titanic_data["fare"] < lower_fare_limit,
lower_fare_limit, titanic_data["fare"]))
```

The following script plots a box plot for the *fare* column of the Titanic dataset after removing outliers using the quantile method.

Script 22:

```
sns.boxplot( y='fare', data=titanic_data)
```

The following output shows that the quantile method is not a very good way to find the outliers. Or you may need to increase the threshold for the quantile values to filter more outliers.

Output:

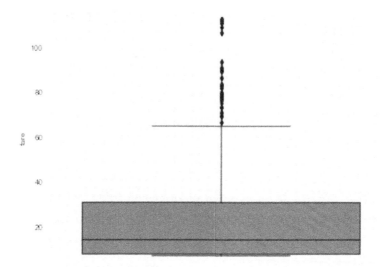

6.6. Outlier Capping using Custom Values

Finally, you can also set the custom values for lower and upper limits to find the outliers. The following script finds the maximum and minimum values for the age column of the Titanic dataset.

Script 23:

```
import matplotlib.pyplot as plt
import seaborn as sns
import pandas as pd
import numpy as np

plt.rcParams["figure.figsize"] = [8,6]

sns.set_style("darkgrid")

titanic_data = sns.load_dataset('titanic')
print(titanic_data.age.max())
print(titanic_data.age.min())
```

Output:

```
80.0
0.42
```

The following script replaces all the values greater than 50 in the *age* column of the Titanic dataset by 50. Similarly, values less than 10 have been arbitrarily replaced by 20.

Script 24:

```
titanic_data["age"]= np.where(titanic_data["age"] > 50, 50,
            np.where(titanic_data["age"] < 10, 10, titanic_
data["age"]))
```

Let's now print the maximum and minimum values for the *age* column of the Titanic dataset.

Script 25:

```
print(titanic_data.age.max())
print(titanic_data.age.min())
```

The output shows 50 and 10 as maximum and minimum values, respectively, for the *age* column.

Output:

```
50.0
10.0
```

Finally, the following script plots the box plot.

Script 26:

```
sns.boxplot( y='age', data=titanic_data)
```

The output shows that outliers have been removed. However, custom capping is not the right approach and should not be used unless necessary, as it can distort the shape of the dataset.

Output:

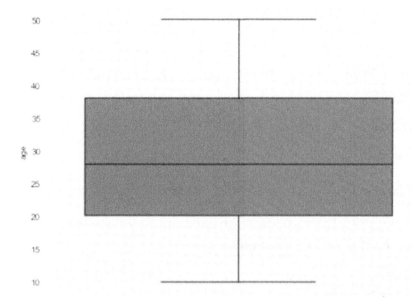

Hands-on Time – Exercise

Now, it is your turn. Follow the instruction in **the exercise below** to check your understanding of outlier handling with Python. The answers to these questions are given at the end of the book.

Exercise 6.1

Question 1:

Which of the following techniques can be used to remove outliers from a dataset?

A. Trimming

B. Censoring

C. Discretization

D. All of the above

Question 2:

What is the IQR distance normally used to cap outliers via IQR?

A. 2.0

B. 3.0

C. 1.5

D. 1.0

Question 3:

What is the quartile distance normally used to cap outliers via mean and standard deviation?

A. 2.0

B. 3.0

C. 1.5

D. 1.0

Exercise 6.2

On the *price* column of the following Diamonds dataset, apply outlier capping via IQR. Display box plot for the *price* column after outlier capping.

```
import matplotlib.pyplot as plt
import seaborn as sns
import pandas as pd
import numpy as np
plt.rcParams["figure.figsize"] = [8,6]
sns.set_style("darkgrid")

diamond_data = sns.load_dataset('diamonds')

diamond_data.head()
```

	carat	cut	color	clarity	depth	table	price	x	y	z
0	0.23	Ideal	E	SI2	61.5	55.0	326	3.95	3.98	2.43
1	0.21	Premium	E	SI1	59.8	61.0	326	3.89	3.84	2.31
2	0.23	Good	E	VS1	56.9	65.0	327	4.05	4.07	2.31
3	0.29	Premium	I	VS2	62.4	58.0	334	4.20	4.23	2.63
4	0.31	Good	J	SI2	63.3	58.0	335	4.34	4.35	2.75

7

Feature Scaling

7.1. Introduction

A dataset can have different attributes. The attributes can have different magnitudes, variances, standard deviations, mean values, etc. For instance, the salary can be in thousands, whereas age is normally a two-digit number. The difference in the scale or magnitude of attributes can actually affect statistical models. Variables with a bigger range dominate those with a smaller range, for linear models. Similarly, the gradient descent algorithm converges faster when variables have similar scales. Feature magnitudes can also affect Euclidean distances.

In this chapter, you will see different feature scaling techniques.

7.2. Standardization

Standardization is the processing of centering the variable at zero and standardizing the data variance to 1. To standardize the dataset, you simply have to subtract each data point from the mean of the datapoint and divide the result by the standard deviation of the data.

Feature scaling is applied to numeric columns only. The following script imports the Titanic dataset and then filters the *age*, fare, and pclass columns. We will be applying feature scaling techniques on these three columns only.

Script 1:

```
import pandas as pd
import matplotlib.pyplot as plt
import numpy as np
import seaborn as sns


plt.rcParams[«figure.figsize»] = [8,6]
sns.set_style(«darkgrid»)

titanic_data = sns.load_dataset('titanic')

titanic_data  = titanic_data[[«age»,»fare»,»pclass»]]
titanic_data.head()
```

Output:

	age	fare	pclass
0	22.0	7.2500	3
1	38.0	71.2833	1
2	26.0	7.9250	3
3	35.0	53.1000	1
4	35.0	8.0500	3

Let's see the mean, std, min, and max values for the *age, fare,* and *pclass* columns.

Script 2:

```
titanic_data.describe()
```

Output:

	age	fare	pclass
count	714.000000	891.000000	891.000000
mean	29.699118	32.204208	2.308642
std	14.526497	49.693429	0.836071
min	0.420000	0.000000	1.000000
25%	20.125000	7.910400	2.000000
50%	28.000000	14.454200	3.000000
75%	38.000000	31.000000	3.000000
max	80.000000	512.329200	3.000000

You can see that the mean, min, and max values for the three columns are very different.

To standardize the data, you can use the `StandardScaler` class from the `sklearn.preprocessing` module. You have to pass the Pandas dataframe to the `fit()` method of the class and then to the `transorm()` method of the class. The following script applies standard scaling on the *age*, *fare*, and *pclass* columns of the Titanic dataset.

Script 3:

```
from sklearn.preprocessing import StandardScaler

scaler = StandardScaler()
scaler.fit(titanic_data)

titanic_data_scaled = scaler.transform(titanic_data)
```

The following script creates a dataframe of the scaled columns and displays the first five rows of the scaled dataset.

Script 4:

```
titanic_data_scaled = pd.DataFrame(titanic_data_scaled,
columns = titanic_data.columns)
titanic_data_scaled.head()
```

You can see from the output that values have been scaled.

Output:

	age	fare	pclass
0	-0.530377	-0.502445	0.827377
1	0.571831	0.786845	-1.566107
2	-0.254825	-0.488854	0.827377
3	0.365167	0.420730	-1.566107
4	0.365167	-0.486337	0.827377

The following script plots a kernel density plot for the unscaled columns.

Script 5:

```
sns.kdeplot(titanic_data['age'])
```

Output:

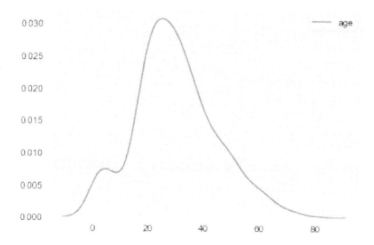

The following script plots a kernel density plot for the scaled columns.

Script 6:

```
sns.kdeplot(titanic_data_scaled['age'])
```

Output:

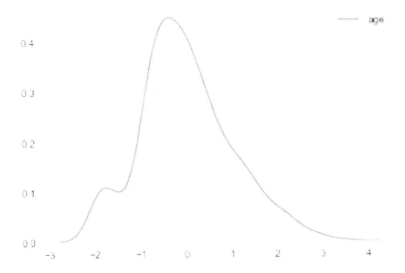

The output from scripts 5 and 6 shows that the standard scaling doesn't actually affect the default data distribution.

7.3. Min/Max Scaling

In min/max scaling, you subtract each value by the minimum value, and then divide the result by the difference of minimum and maximum value in the dataset.

To implement the min/max scaling, you can use the MinMaxScaler class from the sklearn.preprocessing module. You have to pass the Pandas dataframe to the fit() method of the class, and then to the transorm() method of the MinMaxScalerclass. The following script implements min/max scaling on the *age, fare,* and *pclass* columns of the Titanic dataset.

Script 7:

```
from sklearn.preprocessing import MinMaxScaler

scaler = MinMaxScaler()
scaler.fit(titanic_data)

titanic_data_scaled = scaler.transform(titanic_data)
```

The following script creates a dataframe of the scaled columns and displays the first five rows of the scaled dataset.

Script 8:

```
titanic_data_scaled = pd.DataFrame(titanic_data_scaled,
columns = titanic_data.columns)
titanic_data_scaled.head()
```

Output:

	age	fare	pclass
0	0.271174	0.014151	1.0
1	0.472229	0.139136	0.0
2	0.321438	0.015469	1.0
3	0.434531	0.103644	0.0
4	0.434531	0.015713	1.0

Let's plot the kernel density plot to see if the data distribution has changed or not.

Script 9:

```
sns.kdeplot(titanic_data_scaled['age'])
```

Output:

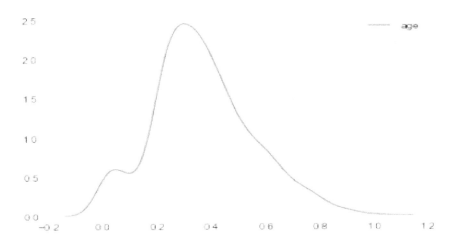

The output shows that the min/max scaling doesn't change the data distribution of the dataset.

7.4. Mean Normalization

Mean normalization is very similar to min/max scaling, except in mean normalization, the mean of the dataset is subtracted from each value, and the result is divided by the range, i.e., the difference between the minimum and maximum values.

The following script calculates the mean values for all the columns.

Script 10:

```
mean_vals = titanic_data.mean(axis=0)
mean_vals
```

Output:

```
age      29.699118
fare     32.204208
pclass    2.308642
dtype: float64
```

The following script finds the range or the difference between the minimum and maximum values for all the columns.

Script 11:

```
range_vals = titanic_data.max(axis=0) - titanic_data.
min(axis=0)
range_vals
```

Output:

```
age      79.5800
fare    512.3292
pclass    2.0000
dtype: float64
```

Finally, the following script applies mean normalization to the complete dataset.

Script 12:

```
titanic_data_scaled = (titanic_data - mean_vals) / range_vals
range_vals
```

Let's plot the kernel density plot to see if the data distribution has been affected or not. Execute the following script:

Script 13:

```
sns.kdeplot(titanic_data_scaled['age'])
```

Output:

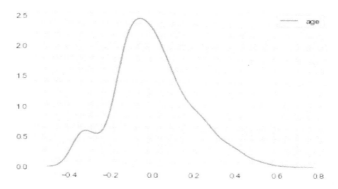

The output shows that the data distribution has not been affected.

7.5. Maximum Absolute Scaling

Maximum absolute scaling is probably the simplest of all the scaling techniques. In maximum absolute scaling, each data point is simply divided by the maximum value.

To implement maximum absolute scaling, you can use the `MaxAbsScaler` class from the `sklearn.preprocessing` module. You have to pass the Pandas dataframe to the `fit()` method of the class and then to the `transorm()` method of the class. The following script applies maximum absolute scaling on the *age, fare*, and *pclass* columns of the Titanic dataset.

Script 14:

```
from sklearn.preprocessing import MaxAbsScaler
scaler = MaxAbsScaler()
scaler.fit(titanic_data)

titanic_data_scaled = scaler.transform(titanic_data)
```

The following script creates a dataframe of the scaled columns and displays the first five rows of the scaled dataset.

Script 15:

```
titanic_data_scaled = pd.DataFrame(titanic_data_scaled,
columns = titanic_data.columns)
titanic_data_scaled.head()
```

Output:

	age	fare	pclass
0	0.2750	0.014151	1.000000
1	0.4750	0.139136	0.333333
2	0.3250	0.015469	1.000000
3	0.4375	0.103644	0.333333
4	0.4375	0.015713	1.000000

Let's plot the kernel density plot to see if the data distribution has been affected by absolute maximum scaling or not. Execute the following script:

Script 16:

```
sns.kdeplot(titanic_data_scaled['age'])
```

Output:

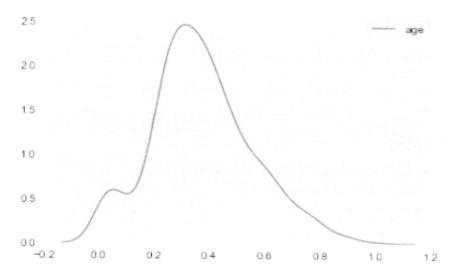

7.6. Median and Quantile Scaling

In median and quantile scaling, the mean of the dataset is subtracted from all the data points, and the result is divided by the difference between the first quartile and the 3rd quartile.

To implement the median and quantile scaling, you can use the `RobustScaler` class from the `sklearn.preprocessing` module. You have to pass the Pandas dataframe to the `fit()` method of the class and then to the `transorm()` method of the class. The following script applies median and quantile scaling on the *age*, *fare*, and *pclass* columns of the Titanic dataset.

Script 17:

```
from sklearn.preprocessing import RobustScaler

scaler = RobustScaler()
scaler.fit(titanic_data)

titanic_data_scaled = scaler.transform(titanic_data)
```

The following script creates a dataframe of the scaled columns and displays the first five rows of the scaled dataset.

Script 18:

```
titanic_data_scaled = pd.DataFrame(titanic_data_scaled,
columns = titanic_data.columns)
titanic_data_scaled.head()
```

Output:

	age	fare	pclass
0	-0.335664	-0.312011	0.0
1	0.559441	2.461242	-2.0
2	-0.111888	-0.282777	0.0
3	0.391608	1.673732	-2.0
4	0.391608	-0.277363	0.0

Let's plot a kernel density plot to see if median and quantile scaling affects the default data distribution or not.

Script 19:

```
sns.kdeplot(titanic_data_scaled['age'])
```

The output shows that the default data distribution is not affected by the median and quantile scaling.

Output:

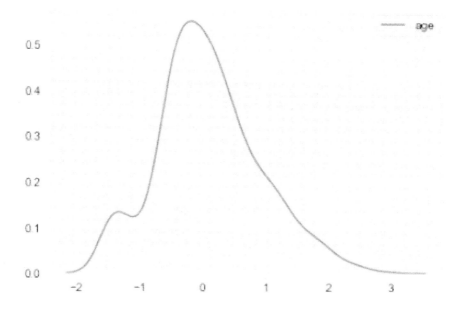

7.7. Vector Unit Length Scaling

In unit length scaling, a new feature vector is created by dividing feature vector by the Manhattan distance (l1 norm), or by the Euclidian distance (l2 norm)

To standardize the data, you can use the `Normalizer`class from the `sklearn.preprocessing` module. You have to first create an object of the Normalizer class. If you pass "l1" as the value for the norm attribute of the constructor, the data will be scaled according to the Manhattan distance. Similarly, if you pass "l2" as the value for the norm attribute, the data will be scaled as per the Euclidean distance. Next, you have to pass the Pandas dataframe to the `fit()` method of the class and then to the `transorm()` method of the class. The following script applies vector unit length scaling with the Manhattan distance on the *age*, *fare*, and *pclass* columns of the Titanic dataset.

Script 20:

```
from sklearn.preprocessing import Normalizer
titanic_data.dropna(inplace =True)
scaler = Normalizer(norm='l1')
scaler.fit(titanic_data)

titanic_data_scaled = scaler.transform(titanic_data)
```

The following script creates a dataframe of the scaled columns and displays the first five rows of the scaled dataset.

Script 21:

```
titanic_data_scaled = pd.DataFrame(titanic_data_scaled,
columns = titanic_data.columns)
titanic_data_scaled.head()
```

Output:

	age	fare	pclass
0	0.682171	0.224806	0.093023
1	0.344567	0.646365	0.009068
2	0.704130	0.214624	0.081246
3	0.392817	0.595960	0.011223
4	0.760043	0.174810	0.065147

Let's plot a kernel density plot to see if median and quantile scaling affects the default data distribution or not.

Script 22:

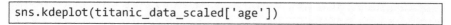

```
sns.kdeplot(titanic_data_scaled['age'])
```

Output:

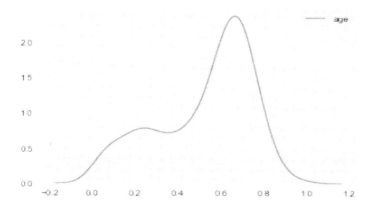

The output shows that the vector unit length scaling actually changes the default data distribution.

Hands-on Time – Exercise

Now, it is your turn. Follow the instruction in **the exercise below** to check your understanding of feature scaling with Python. The answers to these questions are given at the end of the book.

Exercise 7.1

Question 1

After standardization, the mean value of the dataset becomes:

A. 1

B. 0

C. -1

D. None of the above

Question 2

What is the formula to apply mean normalization on the dataset?

A. (values - mean) / (max - min)

B. (value) / (max - min)

C. (value) / (max)

D. None of the above

Question 3

The formula `value/max(values)` is used to implement

A. Min/Max Scaling

B. Maximum Absolute Scaling

C. Standardization

D. Mean Normalization

Exercise 7.2

On the *price* column of the following Diamonds dataset, apply min/max scaling. Display the Kernel density plot for the *price* column after scaling.

```
import matplotlib.pyplot as plt
import seaborn as sns
import pandas as pd
import numpy as np
plt.rcParams["figure.figsize"] = [8,6]
sns.set_style("darkgrid")

diamond_data = sns.load_dataset('diamonds')

diamond_data.head()
```

	carat	cut	color	clarity	depth	table	price	x	y	z
0	0.23	Ideal	E	SI2	61.5	55.0	326	3.95	3.98	2.43
1	0.21	Premium	E	SI1	59.8	61.0	326	3.89	3.84	2.31
2	0.23	Good	E	VS1	56.9	65.0	327	4.05	4.07	2.31
3	0.29	Premium	I	VS2	62.4	58.0	334	4.20	4.23	2.63
4	0.31	Good	J	SI2	63.3	58.0	335	4.34	4.35	2.75

Handling Mixed and DateTime Variables

8.1. Introduction

In sections 2.4 and 2.5 of the second chapter, we briefly reviewed the datatime variables and mixed variables. In this chapter, you will see how to handle datetime data and mixed variables.

8.2. Handling Mixed Values

Mixed variables, as the name suggests, are those variables that contain either a single value of multiple data types or they contain multiple values of different data types.

Let's first see the type of mixed variables that can contain multiple values of different data types. Execute the following script to import the required libraries.

Script 1:

```
import pandas as pd
import matplotlib.pyplot as plt
import numpy as np
import seaborn as sns
```

Next, we will create a Pandas dataframe that will consist of two columns *name* and *Qualification*. The dataset will consist of six rows. Execute the following script to create our dummy dataset.

Script 2:

```
name = ['Jon', 'Nick', 'Ben', 'Sally', 'Alice', 'Josh']
eduation = [9, 'Graduate', 7, 'Graduate', 'PhD', 8]

std = {'name':name,'Qualification':eduation}

student_df = pd.DataFrame(std)
student_df.head()
```

Here is how our dataset looks.

Output:

	name	Qualification
0	Jon	9
1	Nick	Graduate
2	Ben	7
3	Sally	Graduate
4	Alice	PhD

You can see from the above dataset that the *Qualification* column contains integer as well as string values. For instance, the first record contains 9 while the second record contains *Graduate*. This is a type of mixed variable as it can contain data of various types. One of the ways to handle such a variable is to create a new column for each of the unique data types in the original mixed variable. For instance, for the *Qualification* column that contains either string or numerical data, we need to create two columns: one that contains the categorical or string values from the original mixed variable, and the other that contains the numeric values from the original variable. The following script creates a numeric column that will contain the numeric values from the original mixed variable.

Script 3:

```
student_df['q_numeric'] = pd.to_numeric(student_
df["Qualification"],
                    errors='coerce',
                    downcast='integer')
```

Similarly, the following script creates a categorical column that contains the string or categorical values from the original mixed variable. The following script also prints the first five rows after creating new columns.

Script 4:

```
student_df['q_categoric'] = np.where(student_df['q_numeric'].
isnull(),
                    student_df['Qualification'],
                    np.nan)

student_df.head()
```

Output:

	name	Qualification	q_numeric	q_categoric
0	Jon	9	9 0	NaN
1	Nick	Graduate	NaN	Graduate
2	Ben	7	7 0	NaN
3	Sally	Graduate	NaN	Graduate
4	Alice	PhD	NaN	PhD

In the output above, you can see that two new columns, "q_ numeric" and "q_categoric," have been added to the datasets. In the "q_numeric" column, you can see the numeric values from the original *Qualification* column. Similarly, in the "q_ categoric" column, you can see the categorical values from the original *Qualification* column.

As discussed earlier, there is another type of mixed variable where individual values consist of a combination of two or more than two data types.

To see an example of such a variable, you need to import the Titanic dataset. The dataset is available freely on the internet and is also available in the "Data" folder in the book resources folder that is available with the book.

Script 5:

```
titanic_data = pd.read_csv("https://raw.githubusercontent.com/
datasciencedojo/datasets/master/titanic.csv")


titanic_data.head()
```

Output:

	PassengerId	Survived	Pclass	Name	Sex	Age	SibSp	Parch	Ticket	Fare	Cabin	Embarked
0	1	0	3	Braund, Mr. Owen Harris	male	22.0	1	0	A/5 21171	7.2500	NaN	S
1	2	1	1	Cumings, Mrs. John Bradley (Florence Briggs Th...	female	38.0	1	0	PC 17599	71.2833	C85	C
2	3	1	3	Heikkinen, Miss. Laina	female	26.0	0	0	STON/O2. 3101282	7.9250	NaN	S
3	4	1	1	Futrelle, Mrs. Jacques Heath (Lily May Peel)	female	35.0	1	0	113803	53.1000	C123	S
4	5	0	3	Allen, Mr. William Henry	male	35.0	0	0	373450	8.0500	NaN	S

The output shows the first five rows of the Titanic dataset. The Titanic dataset contains information about the passengers who traveled in the famous Titanic ship that sank in 1912. The *Ticket* and *Cabin* columns of the Titanic dataset contain mixed values. Let's filter these two columns and display the first five rows.

Script 6:

```
titanic_data = titanic_data[['Ticket', 'Cabin']]
titanic_data.head()
```

Output:

	Ticket	Cabin
0	A/5 21171	NaN
1	PC 17599	C85
2	STON/O2. 3101282	NaN
3	113803	C123
4	373450	NaN

From the output, you can clearly see that both the *Ticket* and *Cabin* columns contain values that are a combination of numbers and strings. To deal with such mixed variables, you again need to create two new columns. One of the columns will contain the numeric portions of the original mixed values, while the other column will contain the categorical portions of the original mixed values. Execute the following script to create new columns for the Ticket mixed variable.

Script 7:

```
titanic_data ['Ticket_Num'] = titanic_data['Ticket'].str.
extract('(\d+)')
titanic_data ['Ticket_Cat'] = titanic_data['Ticket'].str[0]

titanic_data[['Ticket', 'Ticket_Num', 'Ticket_Cat']].head()
```

Output:

	Ticket	Ticket_Num	Ticket_Cat
0	A/5 21171	5	A
1	PC 17599	17599	P
2	STON/O2. 3101282	2	S
3	113803	113803	1
4	373450	373450	3

From the output, you can see that the newly created "Ticket_ Num" column contains the numeric portion while the "Ticket_ Cat" column contains the first character from the original value. It is important to mention that a space or special character truncates numeric values. Therefore, instead of "5 21171" in the first row, you only see 5 in the corresponding numeric column since there is a space after 5.

8.3. Handling Date Data Type

Date data type, as the name suggests, is a type of data used to represent dates. The following script downloads online data that contains stock prices of Tesla company. The dataset is also available in the Data folder in the books resources folder.

Script 8:

```
tesla_stock = pd.read_csv("https://raw.githubusercontent.com/
plotly/datasets/master/tesla-stock-price.csv")
tesla_stock = tesla_stock.shift(-1)
tesla_stock.dropna(inplace = True)
tesla_stock.head()
```

Output:

	date	close	volume	open	high	low
0	2018/10/15	259.59	6189026.0000	259.06	263.28	254.5367
1	2018/10/12	258.78	7189257.0000	261.00	261.99	252.0100
2	2018/10/11	252.23	8128184.0000	257.53	262.25	249.0300
3	2018/10/10	256.88	12781560.0000	264.61	265.51	247.7700
4	2018/10/09	262.80	12037780.0000	255.25	266.77	253.3000

In the output, the *date* column contains the date data type. However, by default, the Pandas dataframe treats date as string type data. You need to tell the Pandas dataframe to treat the date column as a date time type. This will help us to execute date time type functions on the dataset. To convert string dates to datetime data type values, you need to call the to_date() function and pass it the column that contains date type data as shown below:

Script 9:

```
tesla_stock['date'] = pd.to_datetime(tesla_stock['date'])
```

Once you convert the string column to datetime column type, you can execute datetime functions.

The following script returns the week number of the year in an integer using the date column as the input.

Script 10:

```
tesla_stock['week'] = tesla_stock['date'].dt.week
tesla_stock[['date', 'week']].head()
```

Output:

	date	week
0	2018-10-15	42
1	2018-10-12	41
2	2018-10-11	41
3	2018-10-10	41
4	2018-10-09	41

Similarly, to find the month number, you simply need to call dt.month as shown below:

Script 11:

```
tesla_stock['month'] = tesla_stock['date'].dt.month
tesla_stock[['date', 'month']].head()
```

Output:

	date	month
0	2018-10-15	10
1	2018-10-12	10
2	2018-10-11	10
3	2018-10-10	10
4	2018-10-09	10

To find the day of month in integer, you need to call dt.day on the *date* column as shown below:

Script 12:

```
tesla_stock['day_month'] = tesla_stock['date'].dt.day
tesla_stock[['date', 'day_month']].head()
```

Output:

	date	day_month
0	2018-10-15	15
1	2018-10-12	12
2	2018-10-11	11
3	2018-10-10	10
4	2018-10-09	9

If you want to retrieve the name of the day of the week using the date as input, you can use the dt.weekday_name attribute as shown in the below script:

Script 13:

```
tesla_stock['day_week'] = tesla_stock['date'].dt.day_name()
tesla_stock[['date', 'day_week']].head()
```

Output:

	date	day_week
0	2018-10-15	Monday
1	2018-10-12	Friday
2	2018-10-11	Thursday
3	2018-10-10	Wednesday
4	2018-10-09	Tuesday

Finally, to find the difference between the two dates, you simply need to subtract the two date values. For instance, in the following script, we subtract the date value in the 4th row, i.e., 2018-10-19 from the date value in the 0th row, i.e., 2018-10-15. Since there is a difference of 6 days in the two values, you will see 6 in the output.

Script 14:

```
diff = tesla_stock["date"].iloc[0] - tesla_stock["date"].
iloc[4]
print(tesla_stock["date"].iloc[0])
print(tesla_stock["date"].iloc[4])
print(diff)
```

Output:

```
2018-10-15 00:00:00
2018-10-09 00:00:00
6 days 00:00:00
```

8.4. Handling Time Data Type

In the previous section, you saw date related function. In this section, you will see how to perform several time related functions. We will be using the "bike.csv" dataset for this section. The dataset can be directly downloaded into your application using the following script. The dataset is also available in the Data folder in the book resources.

Script 15:

```
bike_data = pd.read_csv("https://raw.githubusercontent.com/
QROWD/TR/master/datasets/bike.csv")
bike_data.dropna(inplace = True)
bike_data.head()
```

Output:

	user	timestamp	x	y	z	class
0	24c9	2000-01-01 12:00:00	-0.190685	5.475380	8.185829	bike
1	24c9	2000-01-01 12:00:00	-0.299648	5.366417	8.294792	bike
2	24c9	2000-01-01 12:00:00	-0.122583	5.625204	8.485476	bike
3	24c9	2000-01-01 12:00:00	-0.299648	5.570722	8.376513	bike
4	24c9	2000-01-01 12:00:00	-0.476712	5.339176	8.526338	bike

The dataset consists of six columns. However, we are only interested in the *timestamp* column. Like date, you will need to convert the timestamp column to datetime type. Execute the following script to do so:

Script 16:

```
bike_data['timestamp'] = pd.to_datetime(bike_
data['timestamp'])
```

Next, let's print the hour, minute, and second information from the *timestamp* column.

Script 17:

```
bike_data['hour'] = bike_data['timestamp'].dt.hour
bike_data['min'] = bike_data['timestamp'].dt.minute
bike_data['sec'] = bike_data['timestamp'].dt.second

bike_data.shift(-50).head(20)
```

Output:

	user	timestamp	x	y	z	class	hour	min	sec
0	24c9	2000-01-01 12:00:03	10.215261	-3.541291	7.109821	bike	12 0	0 0	3 0
1	24c9	2000-01-01 12:00:03	12.394516	-4.249548	7.722737	bike	12 0	0 0	3 0
2	24c9	2000-01-01 12:00:03	16.807508	-3.241643	6.170018	bike	12 0	0 0	3 0
3	24c9	2000-01-01 12:00:03	16.003908	-1.688923	4.916945	bike	12 0	0 0	3 0
4	24c9	2000-01-01 12:00:03	8.580819	-2.165635	-0.721878	bike	12 0	0 0	3 0
5	24c9	2000-01-01 12:00:03	7.722737	-5.039529	-0.204305	bike	12 0	0 0	3 0
6	24c9	2000-01-01 12:00:03	8.294792	-5.271075	0.980665	bike	12 0	0 0	3 0
7	24c9	2000-01-01 12:00:03	9.370799	-5.271075	0.817221	bike	12 0	0 0	3 0
8	24c9	2000-01-01 12:00:03	8.008764	-4.508335	0.544814	bike	12 0	0 0	3 0
9	24c9	2000-01-01 12:00:03	8.226690	-5.407278	1.784266	bike	12 0	0 0	3 0
10	24c9	2000-01-01 12:00:04	6.183638	-6.891896	-2.329079	bike	12 0	0 0	4 0
11	24c9	2000-01-01 12:00:04	7.314126	-7.790839	-0.626536	bike	12 0	0 0	4 0
12	24c9	2000-01-01 12:00:04	6.687591	-10.365085	2.710449	bike	12 0	0 0	4 0
13	24c9	2000-01-01 12:00:04	6.633110	-11.059722	1.675303	bike	12 0	0 0	4 0
14	24c9	2000-01-01 12:00:04	6.687591	-7.055340	1.893228	bike	12 0	0 0	4 0
15	24c9	2000-01-01 12:00:04	5.652444	-6.782933	-0.953424	bike	12 0	0 0	4 0
16	24c9	2000-01-01 12:00:04	5.883990	6.101916	-0.626536	bike	12 0	0 0	4 0
17	24c9	2000-01-01 12:00:04	3.541291	-6.006573	1.076007	bike	12 0	0 0	4 0
18	24c9	2000-01-01 12:00:04	2.506144	-7.096201	0.926184	bike	12 0	0 0	4 0
19	24c9	2000-01-01 12:00:04	-1.212211	-5.584342	0.653777	bike	12 0	0 0	4 0

In the output, you can see three new columns hour, min, and sec that contain information about the hour, minute, and second, respectively.

The *timestamp* column contains both the date and time information. If you want to fetch the time part only from the *timestamp* column, you can use the **dt.time** attribute as follows:

Script 18:

```
bike_data['time'] = bike_data['timestamp'].dt.time
bike_data.shift(-50).head(20)
```

Output:

	user	timestamp	x	y	z	class	hour	min	sec	time
0	24c9	2000-01-01 12:00:03	10.215261	-3.541291	7.109821	bike	12 0	0 0	3 0	12:00:03
1	24c9	2000-01-01 12:00:03	12.394516	-4.249548	7.722737	bike	12 0	0 0	3 0	12:00:03
2	24c9	2000-01-01 12:00:03	16.807508	-3.241643	6.170018	bike	12 0	0 0	3 0	12:00:03
3	24c9	2000-01-01 12:00:03	16.003908	-1.688923	4.916945	bike	12 0	0 0	3 0	12:00:03
4	24c9	2000-01-01 12:00:03	8.580819	-2.165635	-0.721878	bike	12 0	0 0	3 0	12:00:03
5	24c9	2000-01-01 12:00:03	7.722737	-5.039529	-0.204305	bike	12 0	0 0	3 0	12:00:03
6	24c9	2000-01-01 12:00:03	8.294792	-5.271075	0.980665	bike	12 0	0 0	3 0	12:00:03
7	24c9	2000-01-01 12:00:03	9.370799	-5.271075	0.817221	bike	12 0	0 0	3 0	12:00:03
8	24c9	2000-01-01 12:00:03	8.008764	-4.508335	0.544814	bike	12 0	0 0	3 0	12:00:03
9	24c9	2000-01-01 12:00:03	8.226690	-5.407278	1.784266	bike	12 0	0 0	3 0	12:00:03
10	24c9	2000-01-01 12:00:04	6.183638	-6.891896	-2.329079	bike	12 0	0 0	4 0	12:00:04
11	24c9	2000-01-01 12:00:04	7.314126	-7.790839	-0.626536	bike	12 0	0 0	4 0	12:00:04
12	24c9	2000-01-01 12:00:04	6.687591	-10.365085	2.710449	bike	12 0	0 0	4 0	12:00:04
13	24c9	2000-01-01 12:00:04	6.633110	-11.059722	1.675303	bike	12 0	0 0	4 0	12:00:04
14	24c9	2000-01-01 12:00:04	6.687591	-7.055340	1.893228	bike	12 0	0 0	4 0	12:00:04
15	24c9	2000-01-01 12:00:04	5.652444	-6.782933	-0.953424	bike	12 0	0 0	4 0	12:00:04
16	24c9	2000-01-01 12:00:04	5.883990	-6.101916	-0.626536	bike	12 0	0 0	4 0	12:00:04
17	24c9	2000-01-01 12:00:04	3.541291	-6.006573	1.076007	bike	12 0	0 0	4 0	12:00:04
18	24c9	2000-01-01 12:00:04	2.506144	-7.096201	0.926184	bike	12 0	0 0	4 0	12:00:04
19	24c9	2000-01-01 12:00:04	-1.212211	-5.584342	0.653777	bike	12 0	0 0	4 0	12:00:04

In the output, you can see that a new column, i.e., "time," has been added, which contains the time information only from the "timestamp" column.

Exercise 8.1

Question 1:

Which function is used to convert string type dataframe column to datetime type?

    A. convertToDate()

    B. convertToDateTime()

    C. to_datetime()

    D. None of the above

Question 2:

Which attribute is used to find the day of the week from the datetime type column?

    A. dt.weekday_name

    B. dt_day_week

    C. dt_name_of_weekday

    D. None of the above

Question 3:

Which attribute is used to find the time portion from a datetime type column of a Pandas dataframe?

    A. dt.get_time

    B. dt.show_time

    C. dt.time

    D. dt.display_time

Exercise 8.2

From the Titanic dataset below, the Cabin column contains mixed data. Handle the mixed data in the Cabin column by creating new columns that contain numerical and categorical portion from the original values in the Cabin column.

```
titanic_data = pd.read_csv("https://raw.githubusercontent.com/
datasciencedojo/datasets/master/titanic.csv")
titanic_data.dropna(inplace = True)
titanic_data.head()
```

	PassengerId	Survived	Pclass	Name	Sex	Age	SibSp	Parch	Ticket	Fare	Cabin	Embarked
1	2	1	1	Cumings. Mrs. John Bradley (Florence Briggs Th...	female	38.0	1	0	PC 17599	71.2833	C85	C
3	4	1	1	Futrelle. Mrs. Jacques Heath (Lily May Peel)	female	35.0	1	0	113803	53.1000	C123	S
6	7	0	1	McCarthy. Mr. Timothy J	male	54.0	0	0	17463	51.8625	E46	S
10	11	1	3	Sandstrom. Miss. Marguerite Rut	female	4.0	1	1	PP 9549	16.7000	G6	S
11	12	1	1	Bonnell. Miss. Elizabeth	female	58.0	0	0	113783	26.5500	C103	S

Handling Imbalanced Datasets

9.1. Introduction

An imbalanced dataset is a type of dataset where there is a substantial mismatch between the number of records belonging to different output classes. Imbalanced datasets can greatly affect the performance of statistical models. In this chapter, you will see how to balance the imbalanced datasets.

9.2. Example of Imbalanced Dataset

Let's first see a very simple example of an imbalanced dataset. Execute the following script. It downloads the data of the customers who churned or left a telecommunication company. The dataset is also available in the *Data folder in the book resources.*

Script 1:

```
import pandas as pd
import matplotlib.pyplot as plt
import numpy as np
import seaborn as sns

plt.rcParams["figure.figsize"] = [8,6]
sns.set_style("darkgrid")


churn_data = pd.read_csv("https://raw.githubusercontent.com/
albayraktaroglu/Datasets/master/churn.csv")
```

The dataset contains some categorical columns which we do not need. The following script removes the categorical columns from the dataset.

Script 2:

```
churn_data = churn_data.drop("State", axis = 1)
churn_data = churn_data.drop("Phone", axis = 1)
churn_data = churn_data.drop("VMail Plan", axis = 1)
churn_data = churn_data.drop("Int'l Plan", axis = 1)
```

Let's see how our dataset looks now. Execute the following script.

Script 3:

```
churn_data.head()
```

Output:

	Account Length	Area Code	VMail Message	Day Mins	Day Calls	Day Charge	Eve Mins	Eve Calls	Eve Charge	Night Mins	Night Calls	Night Charge	Intl Mins	Intl Calls	Intl Charge	CustServ Calls	Churn?
0	128	415	25	265.1	110	45.07	197.4	99	16.78	244.7	91	11.01	10.0	3	2.70	1	False.
1	107	415	26	161.6	123	27.47	195.5	103	16.62	254.4	103	11.45	13.7	3	3.70	1	False.
2	137	415	0	243.4	114	41.38	121.2	110	10.30	162.6	104	7.32	12.2	5	3.29	0	False.
3	84	408	0	299.4	71	50.90	61.9	88	5.26	196.9	89	8.86	6.6	7	1.78	2	False.
4	75	415	0	166.7	113	28.34	148.3	122	12.61	186.9	121	8.41	10.1	3	2.73	3	False.

The *Churn?* column, visible on the right most of the above image contains information about whether or not the customer churned after a certain period. Let's first see the shape of our data.

Script 4:

```
churn_data.shape
```

Output:

```
(3333, 17)
```

The above output shows that our dataset contains 3333 rows and 17 columns.

Let's now see the distribution of the data with respect to the customers who churned and those who didn't.

Script 5:

```
sns.countplot(x='Churn?', data=churn_data)
```

Output:

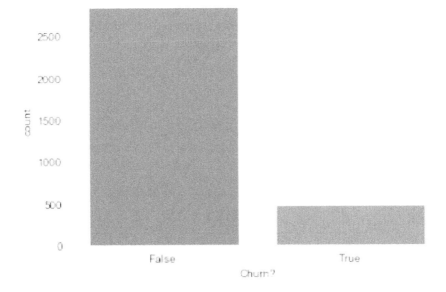

The output clearly shows that one class, i.e., False is in high majority compared to the True. This is a classic example of imbalanced data, and such data can actually affect the performance of machine learning models. Let's see the actual number for the distribution of customer churn.

Script 6:

```
churn_data["Churn?"].value_counts()
```

Output:

```
False.   2850
True.     483
Name: Churn?, dtype: int64
```

The output shows that 2850 customers didn't churn while 483 customers churned the telecom company.

There are two natural ways to balance the dataset. Either remove the records from the majority class or add records to the minority class. Removing data from a majority class is called *down sampling*, and adding data to a minority class is called *up sampling*. Let's first divide our dataset into two sets. One set contains all the records where a customer did not churn while the other dataset contains records that belong to the minority class where customer churn is true.

Script 7:

```
churn_true = churn_data[churn_data["Churn?"] == "True."]
churn_false = churn_data[churn_data["Churn?"] == "False."]
print(churn_true.shape)
print(churn_false.shape)
```

Output:

```
(483, 17)
(2850, 17)
```

9.3. Down Sampling

As I said earlier, to down sample the data, you have to remove the records from the majority class. The following script removes the record from the majority class and makes it equal to the size of the minority class. Here we use the `resample` function from the `sklearn.utils` module.

Script 8:

```
from sklearn.utils import resample
churn_falseds = resample(churn_false,
            replace=True,
            n_samples=len(churn_true),
            random_state=27)
```

Now, if you look at the shape of the churn_falsds, you will see that it contains 483 records, which is equal to the size of the minority class, as shown below.

Script 9:

```
churn_falseds.shape
```

Output:

```
(483, 17)
```

Next, we will concatenate the reduced majority class dataframe with the original minority class dataframe to create a new balanced dataset.

Script 10:

```
churn_downsampled = pd.concat([churn_true, churn_falseds])
```

Now, if you plot the count plot for the *Churn?* column for the newly balanced dataset, you should see equal bars for the two classes.

Script 11:

```
sns.countplot(x='Churn?', data=churn_downsampled)
```

Output:

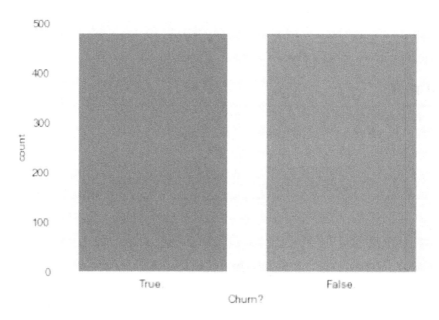

Finally, you can verify the count for both the False and True classes using the value_counts function, as shown below:

Script 12:

```
churn_downsampled["Churn?"].value_counts()
```

Output:

```
True.    483
False.   483
Name: Churn?, dtype: int64
```

The output shows that both the False and True classes have an equal number of records.

9.4. Up Sampling

In up sampling, you simply copy the minority records so that the total minority records become equal to the majority class.

The following script copies the records having Churn? Value of True (minority class) so that the total number of such records become equal to the original number of records where Churn? Value is False (majority class).

Script 13:

```
from sklearn.utils import resample
churn_trueus = resample(churn_true,
            replace=True,
            n_samples=len(churn_false),
            random_state=27)
```

Let's now concatenate the dataframe with up sampled minority class records with the original dataframe that contains majority class records.

Script 14:

```
churn_upsampled = pd.concat([churn_trueus, churn_false])
```

If you plot the count plot, you will see an equal number of records in the *Churn?* column, as shown below:

Script 15:

```
sns.countplot(x='Churn?', data=churn_upsampled)
```

Output:

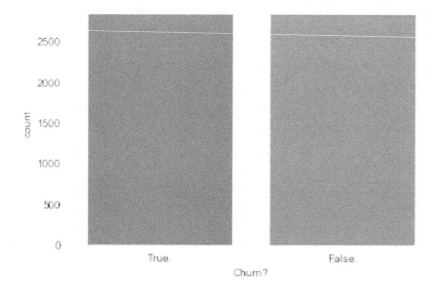

Finally, let's find out the exact number of records where churn is True or False.

Script 16:

```
churn_upsampled["Churn?"].value_counts()
```

Output:

```
False.   2850
True.    2850
Name: Churn?, dtype: int64
```

The output now shows that both the classes have an equal number of records, i.e., 2,850.

9.5. SMOTE Up Sampling

SMOTE stands for Synthetic Minority Oversampling Technique. SMOTE uses the K-Nearest Neighbors algorithm to synthetically generate examples for the minority class.

You can use the imbalanced learn library to apply SMOTE for oversampling. Execute the following script to download the imbalanced learn library.

```
pip install imbalanced-learn
```

To apply SMOTE via the imbalanced learn library, you need to convert the output classes into integers. The following script replaces "True" by 1 and "False" by 0 in the output *Churn?* column.

Script 17:

```
churn_data['Churn?'] = churn_data['Churn?'].map({'True.': 1,
'False.': 0})
```

Next, you need to divide the data into the feature set and the output labels set. The following script divides the data into the features and labels set. We first print the number of values in both classes.

Script 18:

```
y = churn_data[["Churn?"]]
X = churn_data.drop("Churn?", axis = 1)
y["Churn?"].value_counts()
```

Output:

```
0   2850
1    483
Name: Churn?, dtype: int64
```

The output shows that class 0 contains 2,850 records, while class 1 contains 483 records.

Next, to apply SMOTE, you can use the **SMOTE** class from the **imblearn.over_sampling** module. You need to pass the feature and label set to the **fit_resample()** method of the SMOTE class object, as shown below:

Script 19:

```
# install imblearn using the following pip command
# pip install imbalanced-learn

from imblearn.over_sampling import SMOTE

sm = SMOTE(random_state=2)
X_us, y_us = sm.fit_resample(X, y)
```

Now, if you again count the distribution of the *Churn?* column, you should see an equal number of records for both of the classes, as shown below.

Script 20:

```
y_us["Churn?"].value_counts()
```

Output:

```
1   2850
0   2850
Name: Churn?, dtype: int64
```

Exercise 9.1

Look at the following dataset. It is highly imbalanced. Try to up sample the following data sample (the dataset is also available in the Data folder in the book resources) using SMOTE.

```
churn_data = pd.read_csv("https://raw.githubusercontent.com/
IBM/xgboost-smote-detect-fraud/master/data/creditcard.csv")
churn_data.head()
churn_data.Class.value_counts()
```

Final Project – A Complete Data preprocessing Pipeline

1.1. Introduction

In the previous chapters, you saw various data preprocessing and feature engineering techniques that can be used to preprocess data used for various purposes, e.g., machine learning and deep learning. In this section, you will build a complete data preprocessing pipeline that you can use to prepare your data before it can be used by a statistical model. Before we could go on and build our data preprocessing pipeline, let's first see where all the steps involved in creating a machine learning model and where the data preprocessing step comes into play.

1. Raw Data
2. Data Visualization
3. Data preprocessing
4. Feature Selection
5. Training Statistical Models
6. Model Deployment

The first step toward the development and deployment of a machine learning model is the availability of raw data. Once you have raw data, you can visualize or analyze it to extract the information that can be used for data preprocessing. Data visualization can also be performed after data preprocessing steps. Once the dataset has been prepared, the next step is to select the useful features and train the statistical models. Once statistical models are trained, they can be deployed locally or on cloud platforms.

1.2. Data preprocessing

This book is all about preparing data so that it can be used by statistical models. Here, we will revise the steps involved in data preprocessing.

1. Handling datetime and mixed variables
2. Handling missing data
3. Encoding categorical variables
4. Data Discretization
5. Outlier Handling
6. Feature Scaling

The aforementioned six steps are the minimum number of steps that are required to be performed for data preprocessing. All of these steps have been individually explained in this book. The first step, i.e., handling datetime and mixed variables, has been explained in detail in Chapter 8. Missing data handling has been explained in Chapter 3. Categorical variable encoding has been explained in Chapter 4, while data discretization has been covered in Chapter 5. Chapter 6 of this book covers outlier handling, while Chapter 7 deals with feature scaling.

You can add additional steps if you want, such as resampling an imbalanced dataset and so on.

Though we have covered these topics individually, you will need to perform the aforementioned steps in the form of a pipeline that is reproducible and easy to implement and deploy. If you try to perform each of the steps individually, you will run into a very large and difficult to maintain code. Luckily with Pipeline class from Python's Scikit learn library and with Python's Feature Engine library's modules classes for feature engineer, you don't have to execute a huge amount of code for feature engineering. In the next section, you will see how to prepare data using the feature engine library and how to make predictions, all in a single pipeline, with the help of the Pipeline class.

For your reference, we will create a data preprocessing pipeline for both classification and regression problems.

Before you go on and execute the script in the following section, download the Feature Engine library via the following pip command:

```
$ pip install feature-engine
```

1.3. Classification Project

In this section, you will see how to create a data preprocessing pipeline for a classification problem. We will use the Titanic dataset that you have seen in the previous chapters. The task will be to predict if the passenger survived when *Titanic* sank.

The first step is to import the required libraries, as shown below:

Script 1:

```
import pandas as pd
import numpy as np
import matplotlib.pyplot as plt
import seaborn as sns


from sklearn.model_selection import train_test_split
from sklearn.ensemble import RandomForestClassifier
from sklearn.ensemble import RandomForestRegressor
from sklearn.pipeline import Pipeline


from feature_engine import imputation as miss_data_imput
from feature_engine import encoding as cat_encode
```

The following script downloads the Titanic dataset and displays the first five rows of the dataset.

Script 2:

```
titanic_data = sns.load_dataset('titanic')

titanic_data.head()
```

Output:

	survived	pclass	sex	age	sibsp	parch	fare	embarked	class	who	adult_male	deck	embark_town	alive	alone
0	0	3	male	22.0	1	0	7.2500	S	Third	man	True	NaN	Southampton	no	False
1	1	1	female	38.0	1	0	71.2833	C	First	woman	False	C	Cherbourg	yes	False
2	1	3	female	26.0	0	0	7.9250	S	Third	woman	False	NaN	Southampton	yes	True
3	1	1	female	35.0	1	0	53.1000	S	First	woman	False	C	Southampton	yes	False
4	0	3	male	35.0	0	0	8.0500	S	Third	man	True	NaN	Southampton	no	True

For the sake of simplicity, we will only work with the following eight columns of the Titanic dataset in this chapter. The following script filters the columns specified in the "cols" list in the following script:

Script 3:

```
cols = [
'pclass', 'sex', 'age', 'sibsp', 'parch', 'fare','embarked',
'survived']

titanic_data = titanic_data[cols]
```

Let's now again see how our dataset looks like:

Script 4:

```
titanic_data.head()
```

Output:

	pclass	sex	age	sibsp	parch	fare	embarked	survived
0	3	male	22.0	1	0	7.2500	S	0
1	1	female	38.0	1	0	71.2833	C	1
2	3	female	26.0	0	0	7.9250	S	1
3	1	female	35.0	1	0	53.1000	S	1
4	3	male	35.0	0	0	8.0500	S	0

Let's see the data types of different columns in our dataset. To do so, you can use the dtypes attribute, as shown below:

Script 5:

```
titanic_data.dtypes
```

Output:

```
pclass      int64
sex         object
age         float64
sibsp       int64
parch       int64
fare        float64
embarked    object
survived    int64
dtype: object
```

The output shows that except sex and embarked columns, all the remaining columns are of numeric type. The sex and embarked columns are of object (categorical) type.

Let's now check out the ratio of missing values in all the columns.

Script 6:

```
titanic_data.isnull().mean()
```

Output:

```
pclass     0.000000
sex        0.000000
age        0.198653
sibsp      0.000000
parch      0.000000
fare       0.000000
embarked   0.002245
survived   0.000000
dtype: float64
```

The output shows that around 19 percent of the data in the age column is missing while 0.2 percent of the data is missing from the embarked column.

Feature engineering should be applied to the training set, and the features learned from the training set should be used to transform the test set. Let's first divide the data into the training and test sets.

Script 7:

```
X_train, X_test, y_train, y_test = train_test_split(
    titanic_data.drop('survived', axis=1),
    titanic_data['survived'],
    test_size=0.2,
    random_state=42)

X_train.shape, X_test.shape
```

Output:

```
((712, 7), (179, 7))
```

We divide the data into 80 percent training set and 20 percent test set. Hence, the number of rows in the training set is 712, while for the test set, there are 179 data samples.

The next step is to create a pipeline for feature engineering classification. To create a pipeline, you can use the Pipeline class from the sklearn.pipeline module. The constructor of the pipeline class takes a list of objects that perform different types of feature engineering tasks.

In the following script, we pass four objects:

1. *ArbitraryNumberImputer* from the imputer module of the feature engine library,
2. CategoricalImputer from the imputer module of the feature engine library,
3. OrdinalEncoder from the encoding module of the feature engine library, and
4. RandomForestClassifier from the sklearn library.

The ArbitraryNumberImputer Object is used for handling missing numeric data. While the CategoricalVariableImputer handles categorical missing data, the `OrdinalCategoricalEncoder` is used for one hot encoding, and the `RandomForestClassifier` is the algorithm used to perform classification.

Script 8:

```
titanic_data_pipe = Pipeline([


    ('numerical_imputation', miss_data_imput.
ArbitraryNumberImputer(arbitrary_number=-1, variables=['age',
'fare'])),
    ('categorical_imputation', miss_data_imput.
CategoricalImputer(variables=['embarked'])),
    ('categorical_encoder',cat_encode.OrdinalEncoder(encoding_
method='ordered', variables=[ 'sex', 'embarked'])),
    ('rf', RandomForestClassifier(random_state=0))

])
```

Once you create the pipeline, the last step is to apply the pipeline to the training set. To do so, you need to call the `fit()` method, which applies all the steps in the pipeline in a sequence to the training and test set. Once the pipeline functions have been applied to the training set, you can make predictions on training and test sets using the `predict()` method, as shown below:

Script 9:

```
titanic_data_pipe.fit(X_train, y_train)

pred_X_train = titanic_data_pipe.predict(X_train)
pred_X_test = titanic_data_pipe.predict(X_test)
```

Finally, you can evaluate the performance accuracy of the predictions made on the test set via the following script.

Script 10:

```
from sklearn.metrics import classification_report, confusion_
matrix, accuracy_score

print(confusion_matrix(y_test,pred_X_test))
print(classification_report(y_test,pred_X_test))
print(accuracy_score(y_test, pred_X_test))
```

Output:

```
[[90 15]
 [19 55]]
         precision   recall f1-score   support

      0     0.83     0.86    0.84      105
      1     0.79     0.74    0.76      74

  accuracy                   0.81      179
  macro avg     0.81   0.80    0.80      179
weighted avg    0.81   0.81    0.81      179

0.8100558659217877
```

The output shows that with the data preprocessing, we are able to achieve an accuracy of 81.00 percent on the Titanic dataset for the task of survival prediction of passengers.

1.4. Regression Project

In the previous section, you saw how to create a data preprocessing pipeline using feature engineering for classification tasks. In this section, you will create a data preprocessing pipeline for a regression task.

The task is to predict the price of diamonds based on several other attributes. The following script downloads the built-in Titanic dataset.

Script 11:

```
diamond_data = sns.load_dataset('diamonds')

diamond_data.head()
```

Output:

	carat	cut	color	clarity	depth	table	price	x	y	z
0	0.23	Ideal	E	SI2	61.5	55.0	326	3.95	3.98	2.43
1	0.21	Premium	E	SI1	59.8	61.0	326	3.89	3.84	2.31
2	0.23	Good	E	VS1	56.9	65.0	327	4.05	4.07	2.31
3	0.29	Premium	I	VS2	62.4	58.0	334	4.20	4.23	2.63
4	0.31	Good	J	SI2	63.3	58.0	335	4.34	4.35	2.75

Let's now check the data types of different columns in our dataset.

Script 12:

```
diamond_data.dtypes
```

Output:

```
carat     float64
cut        object
color      object
clarity    object
depth     float64
table     float64
price      int64
x        float64
y        float64
z        float64
dtype: object
```

The output shows that the *cut*, *color*, and *clarity* are categorical columns in our dataset, while all of the remaining columns are numeric.

Let's see if our dataset contains any missing values or not.

Script 13:

```
diamond_data.isnull().mean()
```

Output:

```
carat     0.0
cut       0.0
color     0.0
clarity   0.0
depth     0.0
table     0.0
price     0.0
x         0.0
y         0.0
z         0.0
dtype: float64
```

The output shows that the dataset doesn't contain any missing values.

The next step is to divide the data into training and test sets. Execute the following script to do so. The following script will also display the shape of the training and test sets.

Script 14:

```
X_train, X_test, y_train, y_test = train_test_split(
    diamond_data.drop('price', axis=1),
    diamond_data['price'],
    test_size=0.2,
    random_state=42)

X_train.shape, X_test.shape
```

Output:

```
((43152, 9), (10788, 9))
```

The output shows that the training set contains 43,152 records, while the test contains 10,788 records.

The next step is to create a pipeline. Since we do not have any missing data in our dataset, we do not need any missing value imputer. Our dataset contains three categorical columns, i.e., `cut`, `color`, and `clarity`. Therefore, we need the categorical encoder class. Thus, in the pipeline, we only have two objects: OrdinalEncoder for one hot encoding and RandomForestRegressor to predict the prices of diamonds.

Script 15:

```
diamond_data_pipe = Pipeline([


    ('categorical_encoder',
     cat_encode.OrdinalEncoder(encoding_method='ordered',
                    variables=[ 'cut', 'color', 'clarity'])),

    ('rf', RandomForestRegressor(random_state=42))
])
```

Finally, the following script applies the pipeline on the training set, and then the pipeline is used to make price predictions on training, as well as test sets.

Script 16:

```
diamond_data_pipe.fit(X_train, y_train)

pred_X_train = diamond_data_pipe.predict(X_train)
pred_X_test = diamond_data_pipe.predict(X_test)
```

Once you have predicted diamond prices using the pipeline, the last step is to see how good your predictions are. For regression tasks, mean absolute error and mean squared error are some of the most commonly used metrics to evaluate regression problems.

Script 17:

```
from sklearn import metrics

print('Mean Absolute Error:', metrics.mean_absolute_error(y_
test, pred_X_test))
print('Mean Squared Error:', metrics.mean_squared_error(y_
test, pred_X_test))
print('Root Mean Squared Error:', np.sqrt(metrics.mean_
squared_error(y_test, pred_X_test)))
```

Output:

```
Mean Absolute Error: 271.5354506226789
Mean Squared Error: 308115.6650668038
Root Mean Squared Error: 555.0816742307422
```

The output shows the mean absolute error of 271.53, which is less than 10 percent of the mean price value, which is 3,932. This shows that our predictions have been very close to the actual price values.

From the Same Publisher

Python Machine Learning
https://bit.ly/3gcb2iG

Python Deep Learning
https://bit.ly/3gci9Ys

Python Data Visualization
https://bit.ly/3wXqDJI

Python for Data Analysis
https://bit.ly/3wPYEM2

Python Data Preprocessing

https://bit.ly/3fLV3ci

Python for NLP

https://bit.ly/3chlTqm

10 ML Projects Explained from Scratch

https://bit.ly/34KFsDk

Python Scikit-Learn for Beginners

https://bit.ly/3fPbtRf

Data Science
with Python
https://bit.ly/3wVQ5iN

Statistics
with Python
https://bit.ly/3z27KHt

Exercise Solutions

Exercise 2.1

Question 1:

What is the type of *alone* column in the Titanic dataset?

A. Ordinal

B. Continuous

C. Discrete

D. Nominal

Answer: D

Look at the following dataset. It is called the *Tips* dataset. Question 2-4 are based on this Tips dataset:

	total_bill	tip	sex	smoker	day	time	size
0	16.99	1.01	Female	No	Sun	Dinner	2
1	10.34	1.66	Male	No	Sun	Dinner	3
2	21.01	3.50	Male	No	Sun	Dinner	3
3	23.68	3.31	Male	No	Sun	Dinner	2
4	24.59	3.61	Female	No	Sun	Dinner	4

Question 2:

What is the type of *day* column in the above dataset?

    A. Ordinal

    B. Continuous

    C. Discrete

    D. Nominal

Answer: A

Question 3:

Identify the continuous numerical columns in the Tips dataset.

Answer: total_bill, tip

Question 4:

Write the names of the discrete columns in the Tips dataset:

Answer: size

Question 5:

Which plot should be plotted to visualize the probability distribution in a dataset?

    A. Bar Plot

    B. Histogram

    C. Box Plot

    D. Line Plot

Answer: B

Question 6:

The rare label occurrence in a categorical variable can cause _____ in the training set.

    A. Wrong Predictions

    B. Underfitting

    C. Overfitting

    D. None of the above

Answer: C

Exercise 3.1

Question 1:

What is the major disadvantage of mean and median imputation?

    A. Distorts the data distribution

    B. Distorts the data variance

    C. Distorts the data covariance

    D. All of the Above

Answer: D

Question 2:

Which imputation should be used when the data is not missing at random?

    A. Mean and Median Imputation

    B. Arbitrary Value Imputation

    C. End of Distribution Imputation

    D. Missing Value Imputation

Answer: A

Question 3:

How should the end of tail distribution be calculated for normal distribution?

    A. IQR Rule

    B. Mean x 3 Standard deviations

    C. Mean

    D. Median

Answer: B

Exercise 3.2

Replace the missing values in the *deck* column of the Titanic dataset by the most frequently occurring categories in that column. Plot a bar plot for the updated deck column.

Solution:

```
import matplotlib.pyplot as plt
import seaborn as sns

plt.rcParams["figure.figsize"] = [8,6]
sns.set_style("darkgrid")

titanic_data = sns.load_dataset('titanic')

titanic_data = titanic_data[["deck"]]
titanic_data.head()
titanic_data.isnull().mean()

titanic_data.deck.value_counts().sort_values(ascending=False).
plot.bar()
plt.xlabel('deck')
plt.ylabel('Number of Passengers')

titanic_data.deck.mode()

titanic_data.deck.fillna('C', inplace=True)

titanic_data.deck.value_counts().sort_values(ascending=False).
plot.bar()
plt.xlabel('deck')
plt.ylabel('Number of Passengers')
```

Exercise 4.1

Question 1:

Which encoding scheme generally leads to the highest number of columns in the encoded dataset?

 A. Mean Encoding

 B. Ordinal Encoding

 C. One Hot Encoding

 D. All of the Above

Answer: C

Question 2:

Which attribute is set to True to remove the first column from the one-hot encoded columns generated via the get_dummies() method?

 A. drop_first

 B. remove_first

 C. delete_first

 D. None of the above

Answer: A

Question 3:

What is the total number of integer labels in the frequency encoding?

A. One less than the total number of unique labels in the original column

B. Equal to the total number of unique labels in the original column

C. 3

D. None of the above

Answer: B

Exercise 4.2

Apply frequency encoding to the class column of the Titanic dataset:

Solution:

```
import matplotlib.pyplot as plt
import seaborn as sns

plt.rcParams["figure.figsize"] = [8,6]
sns.set_style("darkgrid")

titanic_data = sns.load_dataset('titanic')

titanic_data.head()

titanic_data = titanic_data[["sex", "class", "embark_town"]]
titanic_data.head()

value_counts = titanic_data['class'].value_counts().to_dict()
print(value_counts)

titanic_data['class_freq'] = titanic_data['class'].map(value_
counts)
titanic_data.head()
```

Exercise 5.1

Question 1:

Which of the following discretization scheme is supervised?

    A. K Means Discretization

    B. Decision Tree Discretization

    C. Equal Width Discretization

    D. Equal Frequency Discretization

Answer: B

Question 2:

Which of the following discretization scheme generate bins of equal sizes?

    A. K Means Discretization

    B. Decision Tree Discretization

    C. Equal Frequency Discretization

    D. None of the Above

Answer: D

Question 3:

Which of the following discretization scheme generate bins containing an equal number of samples?

    A. K Means Discretization

    B. Decision Tree Discretization

    C. Equal Frequency Discretization

    D. Equal Width Distribution

Answer: C

Exercise 5.2

Create five bins for the total_bill column of the Tips dataset using equal frequency discretization. Plot a bar plot displaying the frequency of bills per category.

Solution:

```
import matplotlib.pyplot as plt
import seaborn as sns
import pandas as pd
import numpy as np
from sklearn.preprocessing import KBinsDiscretizer
from sklearn.tree import DecisionTreeClassifier

sns.set_style("darkgrid")

tips_data = sns.load_dataset('tips')

tips_data.head()


discretised_bill, bins = pd.qcut(tips_data['total_bill'], 10,
labels=None, retbins=True, precision=3, duplicates='raise')

pd.concat([discretised_bill, tips_data['total_bill']],
axis=1).head(10)

bin_labels = ['Bin_no_' +str(i) for i in range(1,11)]
print(bin_labels)

tips_data['bill_bins'] = pd.cut(x=tips_data['total_bill'],
bins=bins, labels=bin_labels, include_lowest=True)
tips_data.head(10)

tips_data.groupby('bill_bins')['total_bill'].count().plot.
bar()
plt.xticks(rotation=45)
```

Exercise 6.1

Question 1:

Which of the following techniques can be used to remove outliers from a dataset?

    A. Trimming

    B. Censoring

    C. Discretization

    D. All of the above

Answer: D

Question 2:

What is the IQR distance normally used to cap outliers via IQR?

    A. 2.0

    B. 3.0

    C. 1.5

    D. 1.0

Answer: C

Question 3:

What is the quartile distance normally used to cap outliers via mean and standard deviation?

    A. 2.0

    B. 3.0

    C. 1.5

    D. 1.0

Answer: B

Exercise 6.2

On the *price* column of the following Diamonds dataset, apply outlier capping via IQR. Display box plot for the *price* column after outlier capping.

```
import matplotlib.pyplot as plt
import seaborn as sns
import pandas as pd
import numpy as np
plt.rcParams["figure.figsize"] = [8,6]
sns.set_style("darkgrid")

diamond_data = sns.load_dataset('diamonds')

diamond_data.head()
```

	carat	cut	color	clarity	depth	table	price	x	y	z
0	0.23	Ideal	E	SI2	61.5	55.0	326	3.95	3.98	2.43
1	0.21	Premium	E	SI1	59.8	61.0	326	3.89	3.84	2.31
2	0.23	Good	E	VS1	56.9	65.0	327	4.05	4.07	2.31
3	0.29	Premium	I	VS2	62.4	58.0	334	4.20	4.23	2.63
4	0.31	Good	J	SI2	63.3	58.0	335	4.34	4.35	2.75

Solution:

```
IQR = diamond_data["price"].quantile(0.75) - diamond_
data["price"].quantile(0.25)


lower_price_limit = diamond_data["price"].quantile(0.25) -
(IQR * 1.5)
upper_price_limit = diamond_data["price"].quantile(0.75) +
(IQR * 1.5)

print(lower_fare_limit)
print(upper_fare_limit)

diamond_data["price"]= np.where(diamond_data["price"] > upper_
price_limit , upper_price_limit ,
            np.where(diamond_data["price"] < lower_price_limit
, lower_price_limit , diamond_data["price"]))

sns.boxplot( y='price', data=diamond_data)
```

Exercise 7.1

Question 1:

After standardization, the mean value of the dataset becomes:

    A. 1

    B. 0

    C. -1

    D. None of the above

Answer: B

Question 2:

What is the formula to apply mean normalization on the dataset?

    A. (values - mean) / (max - min)

    B. (value) / (max - min)

    C. (value) / (max)

    D. None of the above

Answer: A

Question 3:

The formula `value/max(values)` is used to implement

    A. Min/Max Scaling

    B. Maximum Absolute Scaling

    C. Standardization

    D. Mean Normalization

Answer: B

DEEP LEARNING FUNDAMENTALS FOR BEGINNERS | **233**

Exercise 7.2

On the *price* column of the following Diamonds dataset,
apply min/max scaling. Display the Kernel density plot for
the *price* column after scaling.

```
import matplotlib.pyplot as plt
import seaborn as sns
import pandas as pd
import numpy as np
plt.rcParams["figure.figsize"] = [8,6]
sns.set_style("darkgrid")

diamond_data = sns.load_dataset('diamonds')
diamond_data = diamond_data[['price']]
diamond_data.head()
```

	price
0	326
1	326
2	327
3	334
4	335

Solution:

```
from sklearn.preprocessing import MinMaxScaler

scaler = MinMaxScaler()
scaler.fit(diamond_data)

diamond_data_scaled = scaler.transform(diamond_data)

diamond_data_scaled = pd.DataFrame(diamond_data_scaled,
columns = diamond_data.columns)
diamond_data_scaled.head()

sns.kdeplot(diamond_data_scaled['price'])
```

Exercise 8.1

Question 1:

Which function is used to convert string type dataframe column to datetime type?

A. convertToDate()

B. convertToDateTime()

C. to_datetime()

D. None of the above

Answer: C

Question 2:

Which attribute is used to find the day of the week from the datetime type column?

A. dt.weekday_name

B. dt_day_week

C. dt_name_of_weekday

D. None of the above

Answer: A

Question 3:

Which attribute is used to find the time portion from a datetime type column of a Pandas dataframe?

A. dt.get_time

B. dt.show_time

C. dt.time

D. dt.display_time

Answer: C

Exercise 8.2

From the Titanic dataset below, the *Cabin* column contains mixed data. Handle the mixed data in the *Cabin* column by creating new columns that contain numerical and categorical portion from the original values in the *Cabin* column.

```
titanic_data = pd.read_csv("https://raw.githubusercontent.com/
datasciencedojo/datasets/master/titanic.csv")
titanic_data.dropna(inplace = True)
titanic_data.head()
```

PassengerId	Survived	Pclass	Name	Sex	Age	SibSp	Parch	Ticket	Fare	Cabin	Embarked
1	2	1	1 Cumings, Mrs. John Bradley (Florence Briggs Th...	female	38.0	1	0	PC 17599	71.2833	C85	C
3	4	1	1 Futrelle, Mrs. Jacques Heath (Lily May Peel)	female	35.0	1	0	113803	53.1000	C123	S
6	7	0	1 McCarthy, Mr. Timothy J	male	54.0	0	0	17463	51.8625	E46	S
10	11	1	3 Sandstrom, Miss. Marguerite Rut	female	4.0	1	1	PP 9549	16.7000	G6	S
11	12	1	1 Bonnell, Miss. Elizabeth	female	58.0	0	0	113783	26.5500	C103	S

Solution:

```
titanic_data = titanic_data[['Ticket', 'Cabin']]
titanic_data.head()

titanic_data ['Cabin_N'] = titanic_data['Cabin'].str.
extract('(\d+)')
titanic_data ['Cabin_C'] = titanic_data['Cabin'].str[0]

titanic_data[['Cabin', 'Cabin_N', 'Cabin_C']].head()
```

Exercise 9.1

Look at the following dataset. It is highly imbalanced. Try to up sample the following data (dataset also available in Data folder in the book resources) sample using SMOTE.

```
churn_data = pd.read_csv("https://raw.githubusercontent.com/
IBM/xgboost-smote-detect-fraud/master/data/creditcard.csv")
churn_data.head()
```

Time	V1	V2	V3	V4	V5	V6	V7	V8	V9	...	V21	V22	V23	V24	V25	V26	V27	V28	Amount	Class
0	10	0.385	0.616	-0.874	-0.094	2.925	3.317	0.470	0.538	-0.559	...	0.050	0.238	0.009	0.997	-0.767	-0.492	0.042	-0.054	9.99	0
1	12	-0.752	0.345	2.057	-1.469	-1.158	-0.078	-0.609	0.004	-0.436	...	0.500	1.354	-0.257	-0.065	-0.039	-0.087	-0.181	0.129	15.99	0
2	25	1.114	0.086	0.494	1.336	-0.300	-0.011	-0.119	0.189	0.206	...	-0.053	-0.005	-0.031	0.198	0.565	-0.338	0.029	0.004	4.45	0
3	33	-0.936	0.170	2.746	-1.078	-0.306	0.012	-0.296	0.403	-0.040	...	0.401	1.065	-0.158	0.296	-0.259	0.754	0.047	0.094	9.10	0
4	35	1.199	0.130	0.864	1.003	-0.784	-0.885	-0.041	-0.208	0.392	...	-0.042	0.198	-0.033	1.013	0.559	0.402	-0.006	0.018	0.99	0

Solution:

```
y = churn_data[["Class"]]
X = churn_data.drop("Class", axis = 1)
y["Class"].value_counts()
```

```
from imblearn.over_sampling import SMOTE

sm = SMOTE(random_state=2)
X_us, y_us = sm.fit_resample(X, y)

y_us[«Class»].value_counts()
```

Made in the USA
Middletown, DE
30 December 2022

20769580R00144